Understanding
THE ENDTIMES

Understanding
THE ENDTIMES

What Can We Know About Bible Prophecy?

Understanding The Endtimes
© 2004 RBC Ministries

Discovery House Publishers is affiliated with
RBC Ministries, Grand Rapids, Michigan 49512

Book Design: Sherri Hoffman
Cover Design: Stan Myers

Printed in the United States of America
04 05 06 07 08 09 / DP / 10 9 8 7 6 5 4 3 2 1

Contents

Preface

We live in a day of great turbulence. The news is filled every day with disturbing events from the Middle East. As our attention is pulled to the other side of the globe, we find our own cities and neighborhoods dealing with crises we could never have imagined 20, 30, or 40 years ago. Certainly, we live in perilous times.

The question we must consider is whether these "perilous times" are the same events described by the apostle Paul when he wrote:

> *In the last days perilous times will come: For men will be lovers of themselves, lovers of money, boasters, proud, blasphemers, disobedient to parents, unthankful, unholy, unloving, unforgiving, slanderers, without self-control, brutal, despisers of good, traitors, headstrong, haughty, lovers of pleasure rather than lovers of God, having a form of godliness but denying its power. And from such people turn away! (2 Tim. 3:1-5).*

Are we in the "last days" that Paul referred to? How can we know with any certainty? What does the Bible tell us about what the endtimes will be like? How much has God reserved for His own understanding about the mysterious days of the end? These are questions many people struggle with.

In this volume we have collected Bible teaching from four booklets out of RBC's popular Discovery Series. These particular booklets offer insight and instruction from the Scriptures about world-shaking prophetic events.

As you read and grow in this important area of biblical truth, may you be challenged, strengthened, and encouraged by the God whose eternal purposes will be accomplished.

Bill Crowder
RBC Director of Church Ministries

1

What Can We Know About The Endtimes?

Are the statements in the Bible about the future exact enough for us to know what lies ahead? Or are they too vague, too figurative, or too debatable to be of any real value to us today? What difference does it make whether or not we know ahead of time if it's all going to happen anyway? Let's look to the Bible for the answers to these and other important questions about the future.

—MARTIN R. DE HAAN II

Expectations

A woman in her 9th month of pregnancy.
A college student the week before final exams.
A teenager before his first date.
A man and woman as they say, "I do."
A patient who has been told he has cancer.
A criminal awaiting the judge's sentence.

Do your expectations turn out to be naively optimistic, unduly pessimistic, or surprisingly realistic? In most cases, what makes the difference is whether you acted on the basis of specific knowledge or on unfounded feelings.

Opinions about the future follow the same pattern. To avoid being victimized by false hopes or unrealistic fears, we need to

> Do your expectations turn out to be naively optimistic, unduly pessimistic, or surprisingly realistic?

search out reliable information and live by it.

Many find it hard to know whom to believe. Some predict a nuclear holocaust. Others speak ominously of mass starvation. Many economists are forecasting a worldwide financial collapse. Still others see a peaceful utopia just ahead.

Here are a few excerpts from actual conversations with people who expressed their hopes and fears about the endtimes.

- "I heard some guy on TV talk about the book of Revelation, and it really spooked me."
- "I believe that I will see the end of the earth in my lifetime."

- "I don't see why Jesus would have to come back. If He was the Messiah, He would have done it right then."
- "If the judgment day comes, then I'm going to hell. I enjoy doing the things I'm doing wrong."
- "It's kind of scary to think that the world is going to come to an end someday, but if I have faith there is nothing to be afraid of."
- "I think everybody has the same destiny."
- "The future kind of scares me. I'm afraid of World War 3 and things like that."
- "I think God cares, but I don't think He's controlling things. I think He sees what happens and He hopes for the best."
- "I believe that God controls the future and that Jesus Christ will return just as He promised. I believe in an actual heaven and hell."

Who's right? Which expectations are in line with what we *can* know for sure? In this study, we will be looking to the Bible for answers to our questions about the endtimes.

The Countdown Continues

No amount of effort can stop the clock of history. No mortal, no matter how influential, wealthy, or well-known can break the tyranny of time. Every day that passes, every flash of a digital crystal, brings us closer to the dramatic events predicted in the Bible. We can prepare for the inevitable. We can put time to good use. But we cannot stop it. Not for a moment.

That can be an unsettling thought. The prophetic passages of the Bible are filled with frightening scenes and complicated symbols. There are predictions of the sun going dark and the moon turning to blood. Four terrible horsemen are pictured as riding forth over the earth bringing war, famine, disease, and death. A blasphemous beast will rise out of the sea to shake his fist in the face of God and to bring untold suffering to God's children. A final, cataclysmic war will be fought, and blood will flow 5 feet deep in a valley 200 miles long. Finally, peace will settle over the earth like the warm, benevolent sunshine of spring.

These are frightening, confusing images. And when we read about prophecy, we come across technical terms like the great tribulation, the abomination of desolation, the return of Jesus Christ, the great white throne judgment, and the lake of fire.

What's ahead? How much can we know about the endtimes? Well, not everything, certainly. But the Bible does give us much information. In the pages that follow, we will identify and explain the seven major events of the endtimes.

Christ: Key To The Future

Christ is the center of God's plan for the endtimes.

1. **Return In The Air:** Christ comes back for His own.
2. **Rise Of The Antichrist:** Christ is challenged.
3. **Unparalleled Trouble:** Christ troubles the nations and Israel.

4. **Return To The Earth:** Christ comes to rescue and judge Israel, and to judge the nations.
5. **1,000-Year Reign:** Christ rules the world from an earthly throne.
6. **Final Judgment:** Christ defeats His enemies and judges unbelievers.
7. **New World:** Christ creates a new heaven and a new earth.

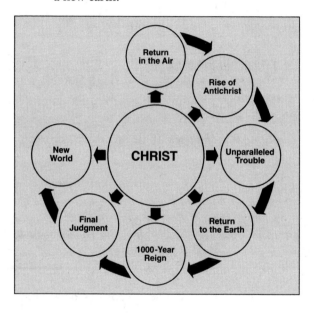

What We Can Know About
The Endtimes

FACT 1: Christ Will Return In The Air For His Own

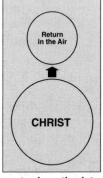

Because Christ can be trusted, we know that He will keep His promise to return for His own. He promised His disciples: "I go to prepare a place for you. And if I go and prepare a place for you, I will come again and receive you to Myself; that where I am, there you may be also" (Jn. 14:2-3).

What Will Happen? This event is described in 1 Thessalonians 4:

> *The Lord Himself will descend from heaven with a shout, with the voice of an archangel, and with the trumpet of God. And the dead in Christ will rise first. Then we who are alive and remain shall be caught up together with them in the clouds to meet the Lord in the air (vv.16-17).*

At a predetermined time, the Son of God will leave the Father's side and descend toward earth. As He does, three mighty sounds will echo across the halls of heaven and sweep over the earth: a shout, the voice of an archangel, and a blast from the trumpet of God. When these sounds are heard, all believers since the time of Christ will be resurrected. The bodies of the

Christians who have died will arise, be transformed, be reunited with their souls, and be taken to Christ's side in the air. Then every living Christian will be removed from the earth, "caught up" to join with the resurrected believers for a great and glorious meeting in the air. Christ will take them to be with Himself, and they will "always be with the Lord" (v.17).

This is also in view in 1 Corinthians 15:51-52, where Paul wrote:

> We shall not all sleep, but we shall all be changed—in a moment, in the twinkling of an eye, at the last trumpet. For the trumpet will sound, and the dead will be raised incorruptible, and we shall be changed.

In a moment of time the earth will be emptied of Christians.

When Will It Take Place? No one really knows when this event will occur. The time is not spelled out in prophecy. We are told instead to maintain an attitude and condition of readiness, for Christ said:

> Therefore you also be ready, for the Son of Man is coming at an hour you do not expect (Mt. 24:44).

Christ taught this attitude of watchfulness in two similar parables recorded in Luke 12. In the first parable (vv.35-40), He likened His coming to the return of the master of the house from a wedding. In the second (vv.42-48), a man has left his household affairs in the hands of a servant.

The key element in both parables is that the day of the master's return could not be known. Because of that, the servants were to maintain constant readiness. The same is true of us as we wait for Christ's return.

This could occur at any moment. That's what the word *imminent* means. But that does not necessarily mean His return will occur

> Some will receive reward at the judgment seat of Christ; others will suffer loss.

soon. Yes, it's *imminent*—it could take place before you take your next breath, but it is not necessarily *immediate*. The Lord could delay His return another few hundred years.

We believe that this event will be the first of the endtime events. It is referred to as "the rapture of the church." The word *rapture* comes from the Latin word *rapere*, which literally means "to seize" or "to catch away." For an explanation of why we believe that the rapture is separate from the second coming of Christ to the earth, please read pages 36 and 37.

The Judgment Seat Of Christ. Those who are taken from the earth will meet Christ in the clouds and go to be with Him. Then they will stand before the Lord in judgment. This event is called the judgment seat of Christ. Paul foresaw it when he wrote:

> *We must all appear before the judgment seat of Christ, that each one may receive the things done in the body, according to what he has done, whether good or bad (2 Cor. 5:10).*

The issue for those at the judgment seat of Christ will not be salvation. They are all God's children— forgiven and adopted on the basis of their acceptance of Christ. The purpose is to determine the degree of reward they receive. They will be called into account and receive what is due them (2 Cor. 5:10). The primary issue will be faithfulness (1 Cor. 4:2,4). This is emphasized in three of our Lord's parables: the worker in the vineyard (Mt. 20:1-16), the talents (Mt. 25:14-30), and the 10 minas (Lk. 19:11-27).

Some will receive reward at the judgment seat of Christ; others will suffer loss (1 Cor. 3:11-15). We are not told just what this will involve. There will be no punishment, for Jesus Christ bore all the penalty for our sin on the cross. We may be shown our shortcomings and failures. We may be reminded of our selfishness and of the sins we did not confess. The "loss" we suffer will be in the receiving of less reward than we could have received.

FACT 2: The Antichrist Will Rise To Power

According to Bible prophecy, the next event on the endtime calendar is the rise of a false christ to world prominence. He is called the Antichrist.

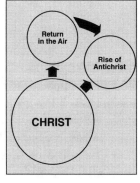

The apostle John said that many false christs would appear (1 Jn. 2:18; 4:3). Claiming to be the Messiah, they will seek and attract many people. Some had already appeared while John was still alive. One day, however, the ultimate impostor will come. He will gather a huge following. He will deceive Israel into signing a false peace treaty (Dan. 9:27). And he will be the cause of untold suffering in the world, especially for the saints.

Here is what the Bible tells us about Antichrist:

- He will receive power from Satan (Rev. 13:2).
- He will receive his throne from Satan (Rev. 13:2).
- He will receive his authority from Satan (Rev. 13:2).
- He will be a ruler (Rev. 6:2).
- His purpose will be conquest (Rev. 6:2).
- He will be guilty of terrible blasphemy (Rev. 13:5).
- He will make a peace treaty with Israel and then cruelly break it (Dan. 9:27).
- He will put himself above everything and everyone (Dan. 11:37).
- He will proclaim himself to be God (2 Th. 2:4).
- He will stage a miraculous "resurrection" (Rev. 13:3).
- He will make war with the saints (Rev. 13:7).
- He will have authority over the nations (Rev. 13:7).
- His number is 666 (Rev. 13:18).
- He will kill millions of believers (Rev. 6:9-11; 7:9-17).
- A false prophet will serve him (Rev. 19:20).
- He will demand that his image be worshiped (Rev. 13:14).

The Antichrist is Satan's counterfeit. As Jesus Christ was sent by the Father, so this false christ will be sent by Satan. The Antichrist is given various descriptive names in the Bible. For example, he is referred to as:

- The Little Horn (Dan. 7:7-28).
- The King Of Fierce Countenance (Dan. 8:23-25).
- The Prince Who Is To Come (Dan. 9:26-27).
- The Willful King (Dan. 11:16,36-38).
- The Man Of Sin (2 Th. 2:3-4).
- The Son Of Perdition (2 Th. 2:3-4).
- The Beast (Rev. 13:1-10).

FACT 3: The Earth Will Experience Unparalleled Trouble

When the Antichrist is revealed, the stage will be set for the terrible events of the tribulation. After this satanically empowered leader rises to prominence, the stage will be set for the most distressing period of all history. For 3½ years he will conduct a reign of 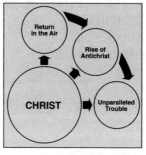 terror, bringing death to multitudes, both Jew and Gentile. But in addition to this reign of terror, the earth will experience unparalleled trouble as God's wrath is poured out on all mankind (Isa. 13:6-11).

The Nations Troubled. The nations will not go unpunished by the hand of God. They will live to hate the day they cast their lot with God's archenemy. For generations their leaders will have rejected God and mocked His Son. A just punishment will befall them in the 7-year period called "the tribulation."

Two sections of the New Testament describe the events of these 7 years: Matthew 24 and Revelation 6–16. These prophetic details indicate how mankind will suffer during this frightening time:

Matthew 24

- false christs
- earthquakes
- wars
- killing
- rumors of war
- betrayal
- nation against nation
- flight
- famines
- pestilences

Revelation 6–16
The Seals (Rev. 6)

1. Antichrist
2. war
3. famine
4. death
5. martyrdom
6. global destruction
7. the trumpets begin

The Trumpets (Rev. 8–9)
1. vegetation destroyed

2. death at sea
3. fresh water poisoned
4. the heavens struck
5. terrible locusts
6. death by demons
7. the bowl judgments begin

The Bowls (Rev. 15–16)

1. ugly sores
2. death of marine life
3. fresh water contaminated
4. unbearable heat
5. darkness and pain
6. demonic hordes
7. earthquake and hail

The suffering and death that will fall on the nations during the tribulation is indescribably horrible. Millions upon millions will die in the terrible outpouring of God's wrath. Yet the majority will not repent. Though they "gnawed their tongues" in agony, they will continue to curse the God of heaven and refuse to trust in Him (Rev. 16:10-11). There will be a great multitude of Gentiles, however, who will turn to God during the tribulation. John refers to them as "a great multitude which no one could number, of all nations, tribes, peoples, and tongues" (Rev. 7:9).

Israel Troubled. There are actually two purposes for the 7 years of tribulation. The first, as we have already seen, is the punishment of the nations. A second is to bring Israel to the place where she can be restored to the position of spiritual favor she once held in God's eyes. Israel will suffer with the nations—only more intensely. This is "the time of Jacob's trouble" prophesied by Jeremiah:

> *Alas! For that day is great, so that none is like it; and it is the time of Jacob's trouble, but he shall be saved out of it (Jer. 30:7).*

The tribulation will be a time of suffering and death for all mankind. But the Jews will be the hardest hit by the terror of those awful days. Zechariah predicted that two-thirds of all Jews on earth will die during the tribulation (13:8-9). But the suffering will bring Israel to repentance.

The prophet Ezekiel described Israel's conversion with these beautiful words:

> *I will take you from among the nations, gather you out of all countries, and bring you into your own land. Then I will sprinkle clean water on you, and you shall be clean; I will cleanse you from all your filthiness and from all your idols. I will give you a new heart and put a new spirit within you; I will take the heart of stone out of your flesh and give you a heart of flesh. I will put My Spirit within you and cause you to walk in My statutes, and you will keep My judgments and do them. Then you shall dwell in the land that I gave to your fathers; you shall be My people, and I will be your God (Ezek. 36:24-28).*

Biblical descriptions of Israel's restoration are also given in Ezekiel 37 (the valley of dry bones) and Zechariah 12:10-11.

The spiritual restoration of Israel as a nation will take place at the return of Jesus Christ to earth at the end of the tribulation. When He returns to rescue them from being annihilated by the Antichrist, they will nationally accept Him as their Messiah and Savior, even though individually a large number of Jews will already have been converted (Rev. 7:1-8).

After hundreds of generations of hardhearted disbelief, the people of Israel will trust in Jesus Christ as their true Messiah. In terrible agony, inflicted by the Antichrist, they will turn in faith to the Lord Jesus. This brings us to the next event in God's program for the endtimes, the return of Jesus Christ to earth.

FACT 4: Christ Will Return To The Earth

As the tribulation draws to a close, the earth will be in turmoil. Millions will have died in war or its aftermath. The Antichrist's hatred of God will focus on the Jews as the 7 years reach their conclusion.

Opposed from the north and east (Dan. 11:44-45), the Antichrist will march his armies into Palestine in preparation for a vast military showdown. Evil spirits will draw the nations together for a final battle on the plains of Megiddo (Rev. 16:12-16).

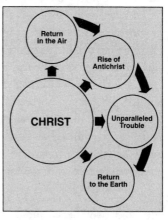

The armies assembled in Palestine will be made up of bloodthirsty men who have resisted God throughout the tribulation. Both sides—the Antichrist and his opponents—will hate the people of God. They will engage in a fierce battle at Armageddon. The fighting will reach Jerusalem, and the Jews living there will suffer horribly (Zech. 14:1-2). A sense of despair will sweep over them as both armies attack them.

Suddenly, when all seems hopeless, the scene will change. Jesus Christ will appear in all His glory and descend to the Mount of Olives. When His feet touch it, the mountain will split in half, forming a vast new valley stretching from the Jordan River to the Mediterranean Sea (Zech. 14:3-9). The Jewish believers will be given superhuman strength to fight the Lord's enemies (Zech. 12:6-9), God will send a plague on the enemy soldiers and their animals (Zech. 14:12,15), and panic will grip the foreign troops, causing them to attack one another (Zech. 14:13).

In Revelation 19:11-21, the apostle John provides us with a beautiful portrait of Christ's second coming. He is depicted astride a white horse, His eyes blazing. The Antichrist will rally the armies of earth to attack Him, but they will be crushed in defeat. Israel will be rescued. The armed hordes of earth will be slain. The Antichrist and his cohort will be thrown into the lake of fire. Satan himself will be bound. And the victorious Christ will prepare to ascend His throne in Jerusalem to rule in peace for 1,000 years.

Those Who Survive The Tribulation. Jesus Christ will hold two special judgments at the close of the tribulation. The first will be for the Jews who survive those terrible days. The prophet Ezekiel described the Lord Jesus as a shepherd standing at the door of a sheepfold. The Jews who have trusted Him will be received into His kingdom; those who rejected Him will not (Ezek. 20:33-44).

A similar judgment will be held for the Gentiles who live through the tribulation. Again, a shepherd metaphor is used to describe Christ. He is pictured as separating the sheep from the goats (Mt. 25:31-46). Believers in Christ (the sheep) will be allowed to enter the millennial kingdom; unbelievers (the goats) will die and await the great white throne judgment (see pp.29-30).

FACT 5: Christ Will Rule The Earth For 1,000 Years

The battle is over. The armed hordes of the earth have been defeated. Just when all seemed lost, Jesus Christ appeared in glory, leading His armies to earth. Before the day ended, the Battle of Armageddon had been won by Him. But the earth is in ruins. Death and destruction lie everywhere. What will happen?

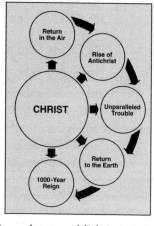

Rather than returning to His Father in heaven, Jesus Christ will erect His throne in Jerusalem, establish it as His capital city, reinstate the Jews as His people, and rule over the entire earth in a 1,000-year reign of peace, prosperity, and righteousness, which we call the millennium (Rev. 20:4-6).

> Rather than returning to His Father in heaven, Jesus Christ will erect His throne in Jerusalem.

The Old Testament prophecies are filled with details about the new government Christ will establish when He returns. Here is what it will be like when the Lord Jesus rules the world:

1. Christ Will Be King.
- The Branch of David will rule (Jer. 23:5).
- Christ will fulfill His prophesied rule (Lk. 1:32-33).
- The believers of the church age will reign with Christ (Rev. 20:4,6).

2. Israel Will Be Prominent.
- Israel will be the favored nation (Isa. 2:1-3).
- Jerusalem will be the capital city (Isa. 60:10-14).
- David's throne will be reestablished (Lk. 1:32).

3. Christ's Rule Will Reflect His Character.
- Justice for everyone (Isa. 2:4).
- All will prosper (Mic. 4:4).
- He will reign in righteousness (Jer. 23:5).
- The earth will be at peace (Zech. 8:4-5).
- People will be safe (Jer. 23:5-6).

4. The Natural World Will Be Transformed.
- Climate will be ideal (Isa. 30:23-26).
- Wild animals will be tame (Isa. 11:6-8).

- Fishing will be great (Ezek. 47:9-10).
- People will have good health (Isa. 35:5-6).
- Life will be lengthened (Isa. 65:19-20,22).
- Trees will provide food and medicine (Ezek. 47:12).

5. *God Will Be Worshiped.*
- His name will be known throughout the world (Mal. 1:11).
- The temple at Jerusalem will be the center of worship (Ezek. 40–48).
- Representatives will come from everywhere (Zech. 14:16).
- All mankind will come (Isa. 66:23).
- The Jews will lead in worship (Isa. 60:10-14).

When Christ rules in the millennial kingdom, His love, justice, mercy, righteousness, and peace will be found throughout the earth. Since people reflect their ruler, the people of the kingdom will reflect the characteristics of their King. During this golden age, the earth will be what God intended it to be.

> When Christ rules in the millennial kingdom, His love, justice, mercy, righteousness, and peace will be found throughout the earth.

FACT 6: Christ Will Abolish Rebellion And Judge Unbelievers

At the end of the 1,000-year reign of Christ on the earth, Satan, who had been locked up during this time, will be released. Immediately gathering a gigantic army of unbelievers together, Satan will lead them

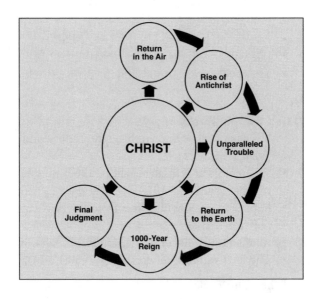

in battle against the Lord. This will be Satan's final act of rebellion.

All Rebellion Abolished. John's description is in Revelation 20:7-10.

> *When the thousand years have expired, Satan will be released from his prison and will go out to deceive the nations which are in the four corners of the earth, Gog and Magog, to gather them together to battle, whose number is as the sand of the sea. They went up on the breadth of the earth and surrounded the camp of the saints and the beloved city. And fire came down from God out of heaven and devoured them. The devil, who deceived them, was cast into the lake of fire and brimstone where the Beast and the False*

Prophet are. And they will be tormented day and night forever and ever.

It had all begun sometime in eternity past, when Lucifer had looked with a jealous eye at the throne of God. In pride he led a rebellion of angels against God and was cast out of heaven (Isa. 14:12-14; Ezek. 28:12-15). From the time of his deception in the Garden until he was cast into the bottomless pit, he has brought immeasurable suffering to mankind. Now, after 1,000 years of confinement, his hatred of God has intensified. He makes one last, desperate attempt to dethrone the Lord. But in spite of all of his power, his fate will be the same as his wicked underlings, the Antichrist and the False Prophet—everlasting torment in hell.

All Unbelievers Judged. When Satan's last rebellion is smashed, it will be time for the final judgment. A new heaven and a new earth will soon be appearing, and the last details of earth-business must be taken care of. This judgment will occur at the great white throne of God (Rev. 20:11-15).

We are told that "the dead, small and great," (v.12) will stand before the throne. Unbelievers of Old Testament days, the church age, the tribulation, and the millennium will be there as the books are opened. No one will escape, for "the sea . . . and Death and Hades" (v.13) will give up their inhabitants. The outcome will not be in question. Those who rejected God's offer of salvation in Christ will have sealed their own fate. Their names will not be found in the Lamb's Book of Life. They will be cast into the lake of fire, which is already inhabited by Satan, Antichrist, and the False Prophet. This is the second death—eternal death.

These are not pleasant thoughts. We don't like the idea of eternal suffering. The idea of flames and anguish appalls us. But remember, these are people who intentionally and willfully chose not to trust in Christ. They turned their backs on God's grace, deciding to leave Him out of their lives. It was their own choice.

God is not vengeful and capricious. He does not cause suffering just for the sport of it. His judgment stems from His holiness,

> God is not vengeful and capricious. His judgment stems from His holiness.

and He is absolutely righteous and holy. No one will receive one bit more or less than he deserves, because God can only judge rightly.

When questions of eternal suffering disturb us, let's remember the words of Abraham: "Shall not the Judge of all the earth do right?" (Gen. 18:25). Then, in faith, we can leave it squarely in His hands.

FACT 7: A New World Will Be Created

We come now to the final event on God's prophetic timetable—which, like a commencement, is more of a beginning than an ending. That which begins with the new world will last from that point on—forever. From the ruins of the old heavens and earth, God will bring into existence an eternal new world free from evil, free from deceit, free from all the harmful, debilitating things that have marred the earth since Adam's sin.

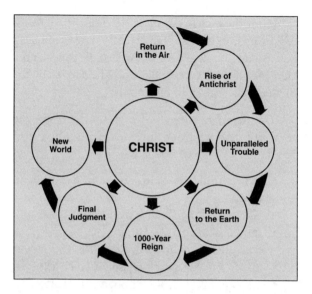

The prophetic books are filled with information about the millennial kingdom, but they tell us very little about the new world to come. Most of our information comes from Revelation 21–22. It begins:

I saw a new heaven and a new earth, for the first heaven and the first earth had passed away (Rev. 21:1).

What will happen to the old world-system? It will be burned to ashes in the aftermath of Satan's final attack (Rev. 20:7-10). Peter described it as follows:

The day of the Lord will come as a thief in the night, in which the heavens will pass away with a great noise, and the elements will melt with fervent heat, but the earth and the works that are in it will be burned up (2 Pet. 3:10).

From these charred, smoking ruins, the Creator will bring into existence an eternal home of amazing beauty and grandeur for His own. As we consider the elements of this new world, we will be dazzled by the picture that appears in our minds.

The New Jerusalem. In his vision, John saw the holy city descend from heaven. He described it in Revelation 21 and 22 as follows:

- as beautiful as a bride dressed for her husband (21:2)
- where God dwells with men (21:3)
- immense in size (21:16)
- a jeweled foundation (21:19-20)
- a 216-foot-high wall of jasper (21:17-18)
- 12 gates of pearl, always open (21:21,25)
- buildings and streets of gold (21:18,21)
- illuminated by God's glory (21:11,23)
- a crystal river (22:1)
- trees of life for healing (22:2)
- the throne of God (22:3)

The city is also remarkable for what is *not* there. The following things will be missing from our heavenly home:

- no sea (21:1)
- no more curse (22:3)
- no tears (21:4)
- no death (21:4)
- no pain (21:4)
- no sorrow (21:4)

- no night (22:5)
- no temple (21:22)
- no sun (21:23)
- no moon (21:23)
- no impurity (21:27)
- no deceit (21:27)

What a wonderful place! There will be no night because our heavenly home will be illuminated by the glory of God, and the Lamb will be its light (21:23; 22:5). There will be no temple because Christ Himself will be the temple (21:22). We will reign there forever (22:5). We will see the face of God and bear His name on our foreheads (22:4). We will have access forever to the tree of life (22:2,14).

> "Blessed are those who do His commandments, that they may have the right to the tree of life, and may enter through the gates into the [New Jerusalem]."
> —Revelation 22:14

With this description of heaven complete, the Bible comes to an end. When we think of the wonders of that home awaiting us, where the Lord Himself will dwell with us, we can only say with John, "Even so, come, Lord Jesus!" (Rev. 22:20).

What We Can't Know About The Endtimes

No biblical subject brings out the imagination in people more than prophecy. Some people look into the prophetic books and always seem to find things that are sensational. Often their conjectures cannot be supported—either by context or by content. We have been talking in this booklet about end-time events that we know will take place. Let's look now at four things we cannot know about the future, but that people often claim to have special knowledge about.

1. The Date Of Christ's Return. Time and again, self-proclaimed prophets have used Bible statements to support their "findings" that Jesus will return on a certain day or in a certain year. Some of these charlatans have even persuaded their followers to sell their earthly goods, combine their financial resources, and head for the hills to await the Lord's return. But God's Word says clearly, "Therefore you also be ready, for the Son of Man is coming at an hour you do not expect" (Mt. 24:44).

Many Christians fell into the trap of date-setting after Israel became a nation in 1948. They based their conclusion on Matthew 24:32-34, which says that the generation who sees "the fig tree" bud "will by no means pass away till all these things [the events prior to and including Christ's return] take place." Since Israel is pictured as a fig tree in the Old Testament, many believed that the Lord would return within the next generation (40 years). This would date the coming of Christ to the earth sometime before 1988 and the rapture of the church before 1981—obviously not an accurate interpretation of the events.

2. The Identity Of Antichrist. Whenever a popular world leader with charisma, charm, and intelligence appears on the scene, he is tagged by someone as the Antichrist. In a sense, the people who make this kind of prediction are on the right track. The one who will rise to international prominence during the tribulation will indeed have those characteristics. We have no scriptural basis, however, for knowing beforehand who that man will be. That will only become evident when he is revealed to mankind during the tribulation.

3. The United States In Biblical Prophecy. Some find it exciting to think that God may have given the United States special mention in His Book. They claim, for example, that Revelation 18 reveals the United States as commercial Babylon. Yet nothing in the passage specifically requires that conclusion. The evils it mentions are just as true of almost every other civilization on earth as they are of the United States.

4. Specific Details. When prophetic experts go beyond what is clearly revealed in the Bible, they are only speculating. In other words, we have no biblical basis for saying that the world will run out of oil, that the United States faces a dictatorship, that paper money will be abolished, or that the number 666 is a computer number. There is a danger in seeing every current event as a fulfillment of prophecy. Details like these are not revealed in the Scriptures.

The Two Phases Of Christ's Return

The endtimes are more easily understood when a distinction is made between the coming of Christ in the air to remove His church and the coming of Christ to the earth to rescue Israel and set up His kingdom. These are the two phases of Christ's return. This distinction is based on the following evidence:

1. Imminency. The Bible clearly teaches that Christ could return at any time. But it also teaches that certain catastrophic events will take place during the tribulation, prior to His return—putting the Lord's people in a state of readiness and expectation. This problem can be resolved if the coming of Christ is seen in two phases. His coming in the air will be sudden and without warning, but His coming to the earth will be expected by those who are alive during the tribulation and who know the biblical record.

2. Israel And The Church. Israel and the church are two distinct entities, with distinct makeup, identity, and destiny. Israel is a nation; the church is made up of people of all nations (including Israel) who put their faith in Christ. Israel is promised prosperity and fulfillment on earth; the church is promised blessings in heavenly places.

3. The Removal Of The Restrainer. In 2 Thessalonians 2:7 we are told that the way will not be clear for last-day events until a "restrainer" is taken away. It seems very probable that this "restrainer" is the Holy Spirit as He indwells individual members of the church. The removal of these persons, referred to by

Christ as the "salt of the earth" and the "light of the world," would clear the way for a worldwide deception.

4. Differing Descriptions Of Christ's Coming. First Thessalonians 4:17 pictures Christ coming in the clouds to "catch up" His people to meet with Him in the air, but Zechariah 14:5 and Revelation 19:14 picture Him as coming to the earth with His people.

5. The Church Not Destined For God's Wrath. Revelation 3:10 indicates that the church is not destined for "the hour of trial which shall come upon the whole world." Scripture speaks of "the time of Jacob's trouble" (Jer. 30:7) as that future time when Israel will be brought to her knees in preparation for the coming of her Messiah. Israel will suffer before her restoration, but 1 Thessalonians 5:9 indicates that the church will escape that day of God's wrath.

6. The State Of The Kingdom Inhabitants. According to 1 Corinthians 15:51, all the righteous will be changed. And Matthew 25:41-46 says that all the unrighteous will be sent into everlasting punishment. If there were no distinction between the two phases of Christ's coming, only glorified, transformed believers would be left to inhabit the kingdom. This doesn't seem possible, because children will be born in the millennium (Isa. 11:6-8). And more important, who does Satan lead in worldwide rebellion against Christ at the end of the millennium if not those unbelievers born during the 1,000 years? Initially, only believers will inhabit the kingdom (Ezek. 20:33-44; Mt. 25:31-46).

Why Study Prophecy?

1. It Promotes Love And Respect For God's Word.
An understanding of the Scriptures shows that God
has fulfilled amazing prophecies in the past. This
assures us that He will also fulfill those that predict
the endtimes. Furthermore, a detailed study of the
prophetic Scriptures is bound to give us a greater
understanding of all Bible truth and a deeper appre-
ciation for God's Word.

2. It Promotes Watchfulness And Purity. It will
motivate us to be ready for the any-moment return of
Jesus Christ. Our Lord Himself emphasized this when
He referred to Noah, to the faithful servant, to the 10
virgins, and to the talents (Mt. 24:36–25:30).

The apostle John exhorted us to be faithful, so
that when our Lord appears we will be confident and
unashamed (1 Jn. 2:28). He went on to say, "Everyone who has this hope in Him purifies himself, just as
He is pure" (3:3).

3. It Promotes A Philosophy Of History. Even
though prophecy does not give us an exactly detailed
prewritten history, it does lay out the future course for
man and the earth. It tells us that the life God created
on earth is worthwhile. It shows that God has specific
plans for man and for our planet. He will correct the
injustices; He will right the wrongs; He will rid the
world of evil. The long, arduous course of human
history will climax in a golden age of universal peace,
prosperity, and righteousness that will exceed our
fondest dreams.

"My Life Was Turned Around"

Clair Hess, senior editor of RBC Ministries, tells how his fear of the second coming of Christ was changed to joyful expectation through a correct understanding of the Bible teaching about endtime events.

One of the memories of my childhood and teen years is not pleasant; in fact, it is a recollection of fear. I remember actually trembling at the thought that the "end of the world" might be near.

I don't recall hearing much teaching as a boy about the rapture, the glorious appearing of Christ, or the millennium. Instead, the people I worshiped with placed an emphasis on the earth burning up with great heat, the sun being darkened, and the moon turning to blood. These images seared my mind with fear, dimmed my interest in the second coming, and drained any assurance I had that Christ would protect His own from the coming tribulation.

When I did hear a message about the Lord's return, I was afraid that I would be left behind. I came home one day after school and found no one there. I was petrified! I was sure that the Lord had come, and that I was the only one in my family who

> "When I did hear a message about the Lord's return, I was afraid that I would be left behind."

was left to face the horrors of the end of time. I had not been taught that because I had received Christ as my Savior I was really safe—for time and eternity.

Although I knew that heaven is the final home of the Christian (and surely everyone wanted to go there, not to the other place), it seemed that only old people spoke of it. No one was really in any hurry to get there. Songs portrayed the beauties and wonders of the "home over there," but they were sung most often at funerals.

I was secretly hoping that Jesus would not come in my lifetime. I had too much I wanted to do. Living seemed more precious, more exciting, than being with Jesus.

After high school, I became interested in the Bible teaching I heard on the radio. I began attending summer gospel tent meetings. I bought a study Bible, and I started reading it with friends. An uncle helped me to understand the sequence of coming events in prophecy. My fears vanished as I read Titus 2:13, "Looking for the blessed hope and glorious appearing of our great God and Savior Jesus Christ."

I learned to live each day in the sure promise of John 14:1-3, where Jesus told us not to be troubled, that He is preparing a place for us, and that He will come back to take us to be with Him.

> "Christ, who loved me and gave Himself for me, is coming. It may be today! Life is more exhilarating now. Each day is an adventure."

As I've grown older, some of my loved ones and friends have been called to their heavenly home. They have gone to be "with Christ, which is far better" (Phil. 1:23). I know the Lord more intimately now, and heaven seems much closer than it did before. I would be glad if He came today.

Christ, who loved me and gave Himself for me, is coming. It may be today! Life is more exhilarating now. Each day is an adventure. Yes, an understanding of God's program for the future has turned my life around.

What Does This Mean To Me?

We have answered the question, "What can we know about the endtimes?" Using the Bible as our guide, we have surveyed what God has revealed about the end of this age and the ages to come. We have looked in on scenes of indescribable bloodshed, horror, and death. And we have had a glimpse of bliss and goodness that surpasses human comprehension.

If you have trusted in Christ as your Lord and Savior, you can have confidence about the future. A day is coming, perhaps soon, when the Lord will return for you. Then you will return with Christ to share in His millennial rule. And after the thousand years are over, you will live with Him in a new world forever in a life of happiness and fulfillment that centers on the Lord Jesus.

But if you are not a Christian, the future is not so promising. The wrath of God will be poured out on the earth, and on you, in a time of terrible war, disease, and famine. And beyond that lies the second death—a fate every bit as real for the unbeliever as heaven is for the person who trusts in Christ.

The countdown continues. The time of opportunity is now. Make your decision. Trust Christ today. Believing that He died to pay the penalty for your sins, ask Him to save you. He has promised that He would. Then, when you

The time of opportunity is now. Make your decision. Trust Christ today.

have done so, your future will be secure—both in this life and in the ages to come.

2

What Can We Know About The Antichrist?

Who or what is this personification of evil identified in Scripture by the code number 666? Is a discussion of the Antichrist nothing more than speculation?

For those who recognize the wisdom of the Bible, the prospect of this "devil in the flesh" is a real and serious issue. Whether or not this evil one has yet been born we don't know, but the Bible says that his spirit is at work in the world right now (1 Jn. 4:3).

This chapter, written by Herb Vander Lugt, gives careful attention to what the Bible says and what it doesn't say about the coming Antichrist whose spirit is already among us. We pray that you will profit, grow, and help others through your knowledge of this enemy of Christ.

—MARTIN R. DE HAAN II

A Timely Subject

A few years ago, several newspapers featured a story about a man who claimed to be the Messiah. He declared that he had gone through a long series of reincarnations, and that this time around he was going to fulfill this crucial role. His spokesman said that he was waiting for just the right moment to go public. He's still waiting.

We certainly don't know when or even if this self-proclaimed messiah will reveal himself. But we who know what the Bible teaches are sure of one thing: He is not the real Messiah! He is an impostor! Jesus spoke of such people when He warned:

> Take heed that no one deceives you. For many will come in My name, saying, "I am the Christ," and will deceive many. . . . Then if anyone says to you, "Look, here is the Christ!" or "There!" do not believe it. For false christs and false prophets will rise and show great signs and wonders to deceive, if possible, even the elect (Mt. 24:4-5,23-24).

Most non-Christians are not ready to talk about an "antichrist," but many people recognize the possibility that we may soon need a world government with a strong man at the head. Some foresee the time when the whole Western world will be under a single monetary system. They point out that nations are becoming increasingly dependent on one another. They also express the fear that small countries may build nuclear weapons if they can get the necessary materials. The well-known economist/theologian

Jacques Ellul, for example, has insisted that we are rapidly approaching the time when all purchases of raw materials will be cleared through a central computer. He sees this as necessary to prevent irresponsible people from producing the kinds of weapons that would give them awesome and frightening power.

Whether we like it or not, we are headed toward increasing internationalism. Whether we like it or not, we may someday find ourselves unable to purchase certain products without having our transaction go through a giant international computer. Whether we like it or not, we may see nations banding together under one powerful leader because of their conviction that this is an absolute necessity for human survival.

> The Bible tells us that the time is coming when the Western world will be united under an incredibly intelligent, tremendously dynamic, awesomely powerful, but frighteningly evil man.

All this doesn't surprise Christians who are acquainted with the prophetic Scriptures. The Bible tells us that the time is coming when the Western world will be united under an incredibly intelligent, tremendously dynamic, awesomely powerful, but frighteningly evil man.

What Are People Saying?

Many churchgoers are intrigued by the biblical teaching about Antichrist. When we asked a number of people if they had any ideas about Antichrist, we received a wide variety of responses.

Here are a few of their ideas about what they expect Antichrist to be:

A Winsome Religious Leader. "Antichrist will probably start out as a religious TV personality. He will have a great deal of charisma and rise to power on the strength of right-wing politics and fundamental Christianity. After he achieves his position, he will show his true colors and reveal his hatred of Christ and everything He stands for."

Someone Like Jesus. "Antichrist will be a Jew about 30 years of age when he begins his rise to power. He will proclaim a new religion and perform miracles like Jesus did. But unlike Jesus, he will reach for and achieve political power."

A New-Age Advocate. "Antichrist will hold to a religion that teaches reincarnation, astral projection, communication with the dead, and a kind of pantheism that says we are all gods."

A Homosexual. "According to the Bible, he won't have any desire for women. So he will probably be a homosexual. The current strong emphasis on 'gay rights' is preparing the way for him."

A Philosophy. "Antichrist will not be an individual, but will be a prevailing philosophy that emphasizes human freedom in moral matters and calls for toleration toward all kinds of religious ideas except true Christianity."

What Does The Bible Say?

Antichrists have been present for more than 1,900 years. The apostle John declared that "even now many antichrists have come" (1 Jn. 2:18). He also warned against "the spirit of the Antichrist, which . . . is now already in the world" (1 Jn. 4:3).

Antichrists may be false christs, men like those Jesus warned about when He said that they would come in His name, saying, "I am the Christ" (Mt. 24:5). Antichrists can also be open enemies, people who hate the gospel and refer to Jesus Christ as "a misguided zealot," "an unsuccessful revolutionary," or "a monumental fraud."

A Bible study that focuses on this subject is not just speculation about the future. It can be very practical, telling us how to face the antichrists and the spirit of Antichrist that is in the world today.

Revelation 13:18 assigns the number 666 to Antichrist, so we have organized our study around three sixes: (1) 6 things we know about him; (2) 6 things we don't know; and (3) 6 things we should do.

6	6	6
What We Know	What We Don't Know	What We Should Do

The Number 666. A time is coming when no one will be able to buy or sell unless he wears some kind of mark that includes 666 (Rev. 13:17-18).

The number 666 shows up from time to time on social security checks, credit cards, and computer printouts. Every time it does, it excites some people. They see it as a sign that we are at the point of Christ's return. Rumors have even been spread that a huge computer in Brussels is being fed information on every living person, and that each of us will be given a number that will include the digits 666. This has resulted in an avalanche of protest letters to government and industry leaders.

"Let him who has understanding calculate the number of the beast" (Rev. 13:18). This admonition has been an excuse for many word games. Using the numerical equivalents of Hebrew, Latin, and Greek letters, people have made the proper names of certain infamous individuals add up to 666. For example, in Hebrew the letter K equals 100 and S equals 60. Employing all three languages if necessary, theorists have suggested the names Nero, Caligula, Napoleon, Kaiser Wilhelm, Mussolini, Hitler, Stalin, and others. Some of the early church fathers believed that the apostle John was making a veiled reference to Nero to help the church avoid needless persecution. The church fathers said that Nero would be resurrected to become the future Antichrist. But few scholars today believe that John had a proper name in mind.

> "The Antichrist is coming, even now many antichrists have come, by which we know that it is the last hour." —1 John 2:18

Dr. John Walvoord writes: "Probably the simplest explanation here is the best. . . . Six in the Scripture is man's number. He was to work 6 days and rest the seventh. The image of Nebuchadnezzar was 60 cubits high and 6 cubits broad. Whatever may be the deeper meaning of the number, it implies that this title referring to the first beast, Satan's masterpiece, limits him to man's level, which is far short of the deity of Jesus Christ" (*The Revelation Of Jesus Christ,* Moody Press, 1966, p.210).

Dr. Leon Morris suggests: "It is possible that . . . we should understand the expression purely in the terms of the symbolism of numbers. If we take the sum of the values represented by the letters in the name *Iēsous,* the Greek name *Jesus,* it comes to 888. Each digit is one more than seven, the perfect number. But 666 yields the opposite phenomenon, for each digit falls short. The number may be meant to indicate not an individual, but a persistent falling short. All the more is this likely to be correct if we translated 'it is the number of man' rather than 'a man.' John will then be saying that unregenerate man is persistently evil. He bears the mark of the beast in all that he does. Civilization without Christ is necessarily under the dominion of the evil one" (*Revelation Of St. John,* Eerdmans, first edition 1969, p.174).

We can't be sure about the exact meaning of the number. But we can be reasonably certain that it has something to do with the devil and his two cohorts, the Beast and the False Prophet. All three members of this "infernal trinity" come short of the perfection of God. They are finite and limited. This satanic trinity is a cheap imitation!

6	6	6
What We Know	What We Don't Know	What We Should Do
1A. His Times	1B. The Exact Date	1C. Be Ready

1A. WHAT WE KNOW: *His Times*

Antichrist may be living today! But he probably won't come forward openly as a Christ-hating world dictator until after Jesus has caught up Christians from the earth to be with Him in heaven. This event, described in 1 Thessalonians 4:13-18 and usually called the rapture, could occur at any moment.

Suddenly, without an advance announcement, Christians will hear a trumpet blast heralding Christ's coming for His own. At that instant, believers who have died will be clothed with their new bodies, and living saints will be transformed. Then both will be caught up, removed from the earth.

This dramatic event will probably cause a great deal of chaos and lead many to believe in Jesus Christ. But it will also make multitudes ready to give their unconditional allegiance to a dynamic earthly leader. Paul connected the rapture to the Antichrist, saying that it will remove the one hindrance to the full outbreak of evil and open the door for Antichrist's manifestation to the world. To Christians concerned that they had already entered the great tribulation, he wrote:

> *Let no one deceive you by any means; for that Day will not come unless the falling away comes first, and the man of sin is revealed, the son of perdition, who opposes and exalts himself above all that is called God or that*

is worshiped, so that he sits as God in the temple of God, showing himself that he is God. Do you not remember that when I was still with you I told you these things? And now you know what is restraining, that he may be revealed in his own time. For the mystery of lawlessness is already at work; only He who now restrains will do so until He is taken out of the way. And then the lawless one will be revealed (2 Th. 2:3-8).

Notice the words, "He who now restrains will do so until He is taken out of the way." Most efforts to identify this restrainer have been unsatisfactory. One Bible commentator admitted, "The Christians in Thessalonica knew, but we don't." The passage makes good sense, however, if we view the restrainer as the Holy Spirit working through the church. Through

> "He was given a mouth speaking great things and blasphemies, and he was given authority to continue for forty-two months."
> —Revelation 13:5

believers, the "salt of the earth," He has been restraining the "mystery of iniquity." As soon as the church is removed in the rapture, the way will be open for Antichrist to come to power.

Antichrist's coming could be close at hand because the rapture is an any-moment possibility. Jesus said that the church of every generation should be living in continual expectancy because "the Son of Man is coming at an hour you do not expect" (Mt. 24:44). Antichrist will reveal himself very soon after the rapture.

1B. WHAT WE DON'T KNOW: *The Exact Date*

While we know that the Antichrist will be revealed shortly after the church is removed from the earth in the rapture, we have no way of giving these endtime events a date.

1C. WHAT WE SHOULD DO: *Be Ready*

Being ready for the rapture is the best way we can oppose and overcome present-day antichrists and the spirit of Antichrist. Jesus issued the exhortation, "Therefore you also be ready, for the Son of Man is coming at an hour you do not expect" (Lk. 12:40). The apostle John wrote, "Beloved, now we are children of God; and it has not yet been revealed what we shall be, but we know that when He is revealed, we shall be like Him, for we shall see Him as He is. And everyone who has this hope in Him purifies himself, just as He is pure" (1 Jn. 3:2-3).

A person who wants to be ready for the Lord's return will try to live a pure life. He won't want to do anything he would be ashamed of if Christ were to return. He wouldn't want to be thinking the kind of thoughts he would be ashamed of if he were to be raptured while thinking them.

When we live in continual readiness for the rapture, we will automatically recognize impostors and the enemies of Jesus Christ. That's the promise of 1 John 2:18–3:3. A believer who is living a pure life and keeping in touch with God through prayer and regular study of the Bible possesses an anointing from the Holy Spirit that will keep him from being deceived by antichrists or captured by the spirit of Antichrist.

6	6	6
What We Know	What We Don't Know	What We Should Do
1A. His Times	1B. The Exact Date	1C. Be Ready
2A. His Character	2B. His Identity	2C. Be Discerning

2A. WHAT WE KNOW: *His Character*

The man called Antichrist in the Bible will at first appear to be a friend of Israel and the world's savior. Eventually, however, he will openly reveal his deep hatred for Christ and His people. This hostility will be his most pronounced trait. In the matter of character, he will be deceitful, blasphemous, satanic, hateful and cruel, immoral, and idolatrous.

A Dynamic Deceiver. Antichrist will seem to be a man of peace when he first appears. In Revelation 6:2 he is portrayed as riding on a white horse, wearing a crown, holding a bow without arrows, and achieving great success. He will be hailed as a great emancipator (Rev. 13:3-4). He will be so clever that the nation of Israel will be deceived by him. Jesus warned, "I have come in My Father's name, and you do not receive Me; if another comes in his own name, him you will receive" (Jn. 5:43).

An Arrogant Blasphemer. As soon as Antichrist dares to show his true colors, he will become an open, bold blasphemer. We read, "Then the king shall do according to his own will: he shall exalt and magnify himself above every god, shall speak blasphemies against the God of gods.... He shall regard neither the God [or gods] of his fathers... nor regard any god; for he shall exalt himself above them all" (Dan. 11:36-37).

Paul described him as "the son of perdition, who opposes and exalts himself above all that is called God or that is worshiped, so that he sits as God [or 'a god'] in the temple of God, showing himself that he is God" (2 Th. 2:3-4).

The apostle John said that he will have "a blasphemous name" (Rev. 13:1) and that he will open "his mouth in blasphemy against God, to blaspheme His name, His tabernacle, and those who dwell in heaven" (13:6).

A Diabolical Satanist. This coming Antichrist will be empowered by Satan and will make him an object of worship. Paul declared that Antichrist's coming will be "according to the working of Satan, with . . . lying wonders" (2 Th. 2:9).

Satan will perform a miracle on this coming Antichrist that will have a tremendous impact on mankind. John said that he saw "one of his heads as if it had been mortally wounded, and his deadly wound was healed. And all the world marveled and followed the beast. So they worshiped the dragon who gave authority to the beast; and they worshiped the beast" (Rev. 13:3-4). The beast will come back to life after being declared dead.

A little later, the second beast (Rev. 13:11-18) will call fire down from heaven and animate an image of the first beast. These miracles will serve a diabolical purpose. They will deceive people into rejecting God and worshiping Satan and Antichrist the way we worship the Father and Jesus.

Unspeakably Hateful And Cruel. This future world ruler will reveal his hatred and cruelty in the way he makes war with believers (Rev. 13:7,10). The extent of his hatred and cruelty is indicated by the fact that the great multitude "which no one could number" is identified as martyrs who came out of "the great tribulation" (Rev. 7:9,14). The number executed under his persecution will probably exceed the combined totals killed by the Nazis and the communists during the 20th century. And all of this savagery will be rooted in his hatred for Christ!

Grossly Immoral. Antichrist will reject all the moral standards held by religious people down through the ages. His title is literally "man of lawlessness" (2 Th. 2:3 NIV). His disdain for all the religions of history is indicated in the words, "He will show no regard for the gods of his fathers" (Dan. 11:37 NIV). He will reject everything good in every historical religious system. He will show his hatred for Christ by rebelling against all moral standards.

Another indication of this man's immorality may be implied in the statement that he will have no regard for "the desire of women" (Dan. 11:37). In ancient days this expression might have referred to the god Tammus or Adonis, two names for a god who held special appeal to women. But since it is unlikely that mankind will go back to worshiping the pantheon of Babylonian and Greek gods, these words probably mean that he will express his disdain for "the desire of women" to marry and have children. If so, he may openly advocate homosexuality. This would certainly be an obvious way of showing his enmity toward Jesus Christ.

A Power-Obsessed Idolater. Although Antichrist will contemptuously mock all the religions of history and boldly declare himself to be God, he will privately bring costly gifts in honor of "a god of fortresses" and will carry out his military campaigns with "a foreign god" (Dan. 11:38-39). This may mean that he will be so power-obsessed that he will lavish wealth on his war machine in a manner reminiscent of the way pagans honored their gods. Some scholars go a step further and say that he will border on insanity by actually worshiping his own war machine. In either case, power will be his idol.

In summary, Antichrist's primary characteristic will be his antagonism toward Jesus Christ. He will be hateful, cruel, lawless, and idolatrous. But he will cleverly mask his true self until it suits his purposes to be open in his hostility toward Christ.

2B. WHAT WE DON'T KNOW: *His Identity*

Although we know what kind of man the Antichrist will be, there is no way of knowing who he is prior to his coming to power. If he is in the world today, his identity cannot be determined. All efforts to identify him through the numerical equivalents of the number 666 are futile.

2C. WHAT WE SHOULD DO: *Be Discerning*

Knowing what kind of man Antichrist will be can help us to be discerning about the religious phenomena of our day. We will be able to identify current "antichrists" and "the spirit of the Antichrist" (1 Jn. 2:18; 4:3). A public figure who denies Christ's deity, His substitutionary atonement, or His bodily resurrection represents the spirit of Antichrist. People who claim that they have a messianic role are antichrists, even though they may say many positive things about the Lord Jesus Christ of history. Furthermore, people who mock absolute moral standards represent the spirit of the one the Bible refers to as "the man of lawlessness."

In summary, we cannot identify Antichrist, but we can certainly detect antichrists and the spirit of Antichrist whenever we encounter them.

6	6	6
What We Know	What We Don't Know	What We Should Do
1A. His Times	1B. The Exact Date	1C. Be Ready
2A. His Character	2B. His Identity	2C. Be Discerning
3A. His Strategy	3B. His Nation Or Race	3C. Be Cautious

3A. WHAT WE KNOW: *His Strategy*
Antichrist will gain his position through deception. He will play the role of a wise leader as he climbs his way to the top of the political ladder. He will portray himself as a man of peace and a friend of Israel but turn out to be neither.

A Man Of Peace. The fact that he will appear as a man of peace is indicated in Revelation 6, where he is portrayed as riding on a white horse, carrying a bow without arrows, wearing a victor's crown, and achieving one success after another (vv.1-2). This is a picture of peaceful conquest, likely through international alliances. Multitudes will see him as their redeemer and look on Satan as their god. Revelation 13:4 reads, "So they worshiped the dragon who gave authority to the beast; and they worshiped the beast, saying, 'Who is like the beast? Who is able to make war with him?' "

This peace image will soon be shattered, however. The white horse is followed by a red one, a symbol of revolution and bloodshed (Rev. 6:3-4).

A Friend Of Israel. Antichrist will make a treaty with Israel that will apparently give her people a sense of security. But at the midpoint of this 7-year treaty he will suddenly turn against the Israelites. He will halt their sacrifices and begin to desolate Jerusalem (see Dan. 9:27; Mt. 24:15-22).

3B. WHAT WE DON'T KNOW: *His Nation Or Race*
Although we know what his strategy will be, we cannot know his national origin nor his racial identity. Efforts have been made to find a biblical basis for making him Jewish, Syrian, or a descendant of Ham, but all such speculation is futile.

3C. WHAT WE SHOULD DO: *Be Cautious*
Since Antichrist's strategy will be deception, we should be very cautious about whom we follow. Not everyone who claims to be a man of peace can be trusted. A person may pose as a friend of Israel in public statements and yet be thinking of ways to destroy her.

The world is full of deceivers today. A few years ago a religious man, who at times referred to himself as a pacifist, received high honors as a man of peace—even though he had encouraged some people in his country to take violent action against the government. Religious people may make eloquent appeals to the Western nations about a reduction of weapons, while at the same time they're espousing the cause of communism. Many religionists lend their support to civil rights activists in the name of freedom, but they will fight against right-to-life laws, anti-porn legislation, or mandatory testing to prevent drug abuse or the spread of AIDS. Interestingly, while they cry out for the rights of those who promote lawlessness, they seek to outlaw Christian schools and do all they can to limit the freedom of evangelicals to preach the gospel. They talk about belief in God but promote principles that give liberty to sin. They are deceptive antichrists.

It follows that we should be cautious and not support any religious or political organization until we know what it teaches and whom it represents.

6	6	6
What We Know	What We Don't Know	What We Should Do
1A. His Times	1B. The Exact Date	1C. Be Ready
2A. His Character	2B. His Identity	2C. Be Discerning
3A. His Strategy	3B. His Nation Or Race	3C. Be Cautious
4A. His Cohorts	4B. Their Names	4C. Be Light

4A. WHAT WE KNOW: *His Cohorts*

The Scriptures portray Antichrist, the beast of Revelation 13:1-10, in close association with the dragon of Revelation 12, the "beast coming up out of the earth" (Rev. 13:11-18), and "the great harlot who sits on many waters" (Rev. 17:1).

Satan. Antichrist will receive his position of worldwide authority through the dragon, who is Satan (Rev. 12:9). The devil will give Antichrist "his power, his throne, and great authority" (Rev. 13:2). Through Antichrist, he will receive worship (Rev. 13:4), just as the Father receives worship through the Son (Jn. 5:19-27).

The devil will perform a tremendous miracle by bringing Antichrist back to life from apparent death. We read, "I saw one of his heads as if it had been mortally wounded, and his deadly wound was healed. And all the world marveled and followed the beast" (Rev. 13:3).

The Antichrist is the seventh head of the beast in Revelation 13, and both the seventh and eighth king in Revelation 17:11. Furthermore, he is pictured as coming up out of the abyss (Rev. 11:7; 17:8). It is possible that he will be killed while seeking his position as world leader, be resurrected by Satan, and become the source of wonder to mankind.

The False Prophet. The second accomplice of Antichrist will be the beast portrayed in Revelation 13:11-18. He is called "the false prophet" (Rev. 16:13; 19:20; 20:10). Just as the Holy Spirit glorifies Christ, the false prophet will honor Antichrist. He will perform miracles and signs. His climactic miracle will be that of giving life to an image of Antichrist. This will induce many to worship Antichrist. For those who do not join in this adoration, the false prophet will bring death by execution or slow starvation. He will take control so that no one will be able to buy or sell without a mark indicating loyalty to Antichrist.

The Harlot. The third cohort of Antichrist will be the harlot of Revelation 17. She is pictured as riding on a scarlet beast with seven heads and ten horns. The seven heads are declared to be seven mountains (v.9), probably the city of Rome. The seven heads are also seven kings or kingdoms (v.10). The five fallen ones are Egypt, Assyria, Babylon, Persia, and Greece. The sixth is the Roman Empire of New Testament days. The seventh will be the future restored empire under Antichrist. The eighth may be his kingdom after he is killed and resurrected by the devil. The ten horns will be a federation of Western nations organized by Antichrist during the time of his rise to power.

The harlot of Revelation 17 will be a religious system that probably will have its headquarters in Rome, the city of seven hills. She is identified as "BABYLON THE GREAT, THE MOTHER OF HARLOTS AND OF THE ABOMINATIONS OF THE EARTH" (Rev. 17:5). This title is significant. It was in ancient Babylon that the fertility cult religious system was developed. It spread to Egypt, Assyria, Persia, Greece, and Rome. In all of these cultures, it promoted the same set of gods and godesses under different names. It always had room for more gods. It was popular because it sanctioned and promoted immorality, tolerated a wide variety of beliefs, and produced seemingly supernatural experiences.

The harlot of the endtimes will bring together into one system a merger of occultism, eastern mysticism, pantheism, reincarnation, nature worship, and the like. It probably will tolerate everything except biblical Christianity.

The heads of this ecumenical religion will work closely with Antichrist as he rises to power. But they will not fare very well after Antichrist achieves world power. They will be destroyed by the very ones they helped (Rev. 17:16).

In summary, the dragon (Satan), the beast (Antichrist), and the false prophet will be an unholy trinity. They will imitate the relationship that exists between the Father, the Son, and the Holy Spirit. They will accept the cooperation and help of an ecumenical religious system in exchange for favors. But once they achieve absolute power, they will destroy the false church so that they will have complete freedom to establish their own anti-god regime.

4B. WHAT WE DON'T KNOW: *Their Names*
We know the name of the first cohort of Antichrist. He is Satan. But we cannot attach a name to the false prophet. In this respect we are under the same limitations that we are when we try to identify Antichrist. Furthermore, we cannot point to any religious group and say that it will become the harlot of Revelation 17.

4C. WHAT WE SHOULD DO: *Be Light*
While it is both foolish and futile to identify the coming false prophet or harlot, we can oppose them by being light-bearers. Light in the Bible represents both truth and goodness. Jesus said of believers, "You are the light of the world. . . . Let your light so shine before men, that they may see your good works and glorify your Father in

heaven" (Mt. 5:14,16). Paul wrote, "You were once darkness, but now you are light in the Lord. Walk as children of light" (Eph. 5:8). By shining the light of truth and godliness, we reflect the triune God, who is perfect in love and holiness.

God our Father is "the Holy One" (Isa. 1:4; 5:19,24; 10:20; 12:6). The devil is "the evil one" (Mt. 6:13). God cannot lie (Num. 23:19; Heb. 6:18). Satan is "a liar, and the father of it" (Jn. 8:42-44).

Jesus Christ brought to mankind the fullness of grace and truth (Jn. 1:17). He loved His enemies so much that He laid down His life in the terrible death of Calvary to pay the price for their sins. He was so pure that no one could accuse Him of sin. Antichrist, on the other hand, will be the very antithesis of graciousness, truth, and love. He will be "the man of lawlessness"—cruel, deceitful, and hateful.

> By walking as children of light, we can restrain the forces of evil that represent the spirit of Antichrist.

The Holy Spirit brings spiritual life (Eph. 2:1-4) and transformation (2 Cor. 3:1-18). In those who yield to Him, He produces the fruit of the Spirit: "love, joy, peace, longsuffering, kindness, goodness, faithfulness, gentleness, self-control" (Gal. 5:22). The false prophet will join with Satan and Antichrist in bringing death to saints (Rev. 13:1-18). He will also help his cohorts to persuade a company of earthly leaders to engage in a military campaign, which will bring about their own doom (Rev. 16:12-16).

We who belong to the true and living God represent Him properly when we, through our lives, reflect the light that He is. Paul speaks of this light as revealed in "goodness, righteousness, and truth" (Eph. 5:9). By walking as children of light, we can restrain the forces of evil that represent the spirit of Antichrist. We won't delay the endtime appearance of Antichrist and the false prophet or the harlot, but we can lead people out of the darkness of sin into the light of the gospel.

6	6	6
What We Know	What We Don't Know	What We Should Do
1A. His Times	1B. The Exact Date	1C. Be Ready
2A. His Character	2B. His Identity	2C. Be Discerning
3A. His Strategy	3B. His Nation Or Race	3C. Be Cautious
4A. His Cohorts	4B. Their Names	4C. Be Light
5A. His Domain	5B. The Actual Nations	5C. Be Informed

5A. WHAT WE KNOW: *His Domain*

Antichrist will be the official ruler of the Western world and exercise power over all mankind. He will rule over what may be termed the "revived Roman Empire." The books of Daniel and Revelation give us this information.

According To Daniel 2. This chapter relates the story of a king's dream and a prophet's explanation of it. About 600 BC, Nebuchadnezzar, king of the Babylonian Empire, had a dream in which he saw a huge image. While he was looking at it, he saw a rock—mysteriously cut out of a mountain—roll down the slope, strike the statue on its feet of iron and clay, and smash it to bits.

From what Daniel told the king, and from what history tells us, we know that the head of gold represented Babylon, and that the other sections of the image represented Medo-Persia, Greece, and Rome. Rome, the iron part of the image, gradually deteriorated and divided into two sections. Historically, the western part lasted until AD 476, the eastern part until about 1450.

> This prophecy cannot be literally fulfilled unless the Roman Empire is in place again at the time when Christ returns to the earth.

In the dream, however, the Roman Empire is suddenly destroyed. Therefore, this prophecy cannot be literally fulfilled unless the Roman Empire is in place again at the time when Christ returns to the earth.

This raises some questions. Does this mean that the restored Roman Empire will have the same boundaries that it had in the past? Not necessarily. The geographical limits of empires change. Their capital cities may even change, as happened in the British Empire when London replaced Winchester as the capital during the 13th century. The Roman Empire is equivalent to what we usually call the Western world—those nations that have kept *Corpus Juris Civilis* (the body of Roman law) as the basis of their jurisprudence. We usually think of everything from the Middle East northward, all of Western Europe, and everything in the Americas as the Western world.

According To Revelation 13. The beast of Revelation 13 has ten horns and seven heads. We have already noted that the seven heads represent a succession of great empires. The ten horns, as indicated earlier, represent ten nations that will make up Antichrist's empire. The lion, bear, and leopard in Revelation 13, as in Daniel 7, represent the Babylonian, Medo-Persian, and Greek empires. This vision suggests that Antichrist's final empire will combine the strongest elements of all these ancient kingdoms.

> "The dragon gave him his power, his throne, and great authority.... And all the world marveled and followed the beast."
> —Revelation 13:2-3

5B. WHAT WE DON'T KNOW: *The Actual Nations*

Some people are certain that the European Common Market is a forerunner of Antichrist's kingdom. While it's possible, no one can really know. The number in the Common Market changes from time to time. Furthermore, the ten nations that will be confederates of Antichrist will probably include some from the Middle East, North Africa, and the Americas.

We can't even be sure about the capital city of this coming empire. It may be Rome, Babylon, or a brand-new city. Therefore, all speculation about the exact boundaries of Antichrist's empire, the names of the nations that will compose it, or the identity of the capital are quite useless.

5C. WHAT WE SHOULD DO: *Be Informed*

An intelligent awareness of present-day trends toward internationalization will help us fulfill our role as Christian citizens. It will also heighten our anticipation of Christ's second coming. Of course, not all internationalization is necessarily evil. Free trade lifts the standard of living in many countries. Regulation of materials used to produce nuclear power may become an absolute necessity. But efforts to bring together all people into a secular humanistic view of life by controlling education of children must be opposed.

The fact that we are moving rapidly toward a united world may be an indication that the time of Antichrist is near. With present-day technology, a world ruler could quite easily control all buying and selling. These facts should not alarm us, however. Rather, they should heighten our anticipation of the Lord's return.

6	6	6
What We Know	What We Don't Know	What We Should Do
1A. His Times	1B. The Exact Date	1C. Be Ready
2A. His Character	2B. His Identity	2C. Be Discerning
3A. His Strategy	3B. His Nation Or Race	3C. Be Cautious
4A. His Cohorts	4B. Their Names	4C. Be Light
5A. His Domain	5B. The Actual Nations	5C. Be Informed
6A. His Defeat	6B. The Details Of War	6C. Be Confident

6A. What We Know: *His Defeat*

Antichrist will rule for only a brief time. Then he will be thoroughly defeated. After he breaks his pact with Israel, he will have only 3½ years left (Dan. 9:24-27). Daniel 11:40-45 indicates that before the 3½ years have expired he will face rebellion—one by the "king of the South" and the other by the "king of the North." He will defeat them, sweep through the Middle East, wreak havoc with the Jewish people, hear troubling news from the east and north, and become involved in the battle that will bring about his total destruction.

Zechariah 14 gives us some additional facts of Antichrist's waterloo. His forces will meet their doom while they are pillaging Jerusalem. When the Lord returns to the Mount of Olives, the topography of Israel will suddenly be changed. Frightful plagues will strike the enemy. Godly Israelites will join the armies from heaven in attacking their foes. And the Lord Jesus will bring order out of the chaos.

Revelation tells us that the Euphrates River will be dried up so that "the way of the kings from the east might be prepared" (16:12). Unclean spirits sent by the "infernal trinity" will deceive rulers of nations to gather their armies at the Valley of Megiddo to fight a climactic battle against God (16:13-16). Commercial Babylon will be supernaturally destroyed (ch. 18). And Christ will come down as Leader of the armies of heaven, destroy the enemies, and cast the beast and false prophet into the lake of fire (19:11-21).

6B. WHAT WE DON'T KNOW: *The Details Of War*

While Daniel, Zechariah, and Revelation show Antichrist and his army being thoroughly defeated at Christ's return, they don't put all the pieces together. We can't name the nations that make up the southern and northern alliances in Daniel 11. We can't identify the "kings from the east" (Rev. 16:12). And we can't present a detailed chronology of the War of Armageddon. Many of the details, like those involved in Christ's first coming, will become clear as they are fulfilled.

6C. WHAT WE SHOULD DO: *Be Confident*

While we cannot put everything in place, we can read these prophecies with the confidence that God and His people will triumph! Everything earthly is going to perish, but we who believe are citizens of a world that will last forever. Let's be sure that we give the right answer to Peter's probing question, "Therefore, since all these things will be dissolved, what manner of persons ought you to be in holy conduct and godliness, looking for and hastening the coming of the day of God, because of which the heavens will be dissolved, being on fire, and the elements will melt with fervent heat?" (2 Pet. 3:11-12).

Why Study Prophecy?

After a person has studied the prophecies of the Bible, what has he really gained? What practical value can be derived from information about the future Antichrist?

These questions are worth considering. The fact of the matter is that some people who specialize in Bible prophecy show little real devotion to Christ and rarely try to lead anyone to the Lord Jesus. Their minds are full of information but their hearts are empty. They aren't gaining anything of spiritual value from their

> God would not have included so much prophetic information in the Scriptures if He didn't want us to study it and teach it.

searching of the Scriptures. But it needn't be that way. God would not have included so much prophetic information in the Scriptures if He didn't want us to study it and teach it.

I grew up in a denomination that interpreted prophecy from an amillennial position. In other words, my pastors taught that there will be no future reestablishment of Israel as God's special people, and that the Old Testament prophecies of a golden age—passages like Isaiah 2:1-4; 11:1-16; Jeremiah 23:5-6; Ezekiel 36:1-38—will never be fulfilled because of Israel's rejection of Christ when He came. As a result, many chapters in the Bible were meaningless to me.

I felt uneasy about this. I also found myself arguing with a lay mission worker when he said, "Our pastor sneers at the idea that the nation of Israel has a future, but I keep finding Bible passages indicating that Israel will be regathered and converted." A few years later, while I was reading Ezekiel 36, I saw something I had never seen before. In this passage, God reiterated His promises of Israel's restoration and declared, "I do not do this for your sake, O house of Israel, but for My holy name's sake, which you have profaned among the nations wherever you went" (Ezek. 36:22). This destroyed my idea that Israel, through her sin and unbelief, had forfeited these promised blessings.

I started a more careful reading of the Old Testament prophets and began to see that God certainly does have an earthly program for Israel. I also saw that Israel and the church are distinct entities. Before long, the prophecies of the Old Testament began to come alive. The Word of God became more vital and real to me. As a result, I grew spiritually. I became more conscious of the promise that Jesus is coming again. My conduct improved and my desire to win others to Christ grew!

The study of Bible prophecy can be just a mental exercise—but so can a study of the attributes of God or any other aspect of Bible doctrine. The secret for success is our relationship with God. If we love the Lord, view the Scriptures as His message to us, and desire above all else to know Him more intimately and serve Him more perfectly, we *will* grow through the study of prophecy.

Daniel's Seventieth Week

The time-frame for endtime chronology is found in Daniel 9:24-27, the passage that describes Israel's "seventy weeks." These "weeks" are clearly 7-year periods. The "seventy weeks," therefore, are 490 years. The first 69 "weeks" (483 years) take us from the decree of Artaxerxes in 445 BC (Neh. 2:5-6) until the "cutting off" of the Messiah (Dan. 9:26). This is, by almost universal consent, a reference to Christ's crucifixion. The Romans under Titus fulfilled the rest of verse 26 by destroying Jerusalem and the temple in AD 70.

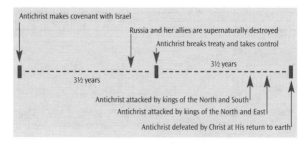

In this passage we encounter the Antichrist—the one called "the prince who is to come." He will "confirm a covenant with many [Daniel's people, the Jews (v.24)] for one week [7 years]." This is the "seventieth week," the time when God will resume His special dealing with Israel. Antichrist, in keeping with his character, will break his treaty after 3½ years ("the middle of the week" [v.27]) and instigate a reign of terror that will desolate the city of Jerusalem. But he will meet his doom when Christ returns to earth.

Antichrist And The Church

Bible students who believe that Jesus Christ could return at any moment to remove believers from the earth (the rapture of the church) are convinced that this will occur before Antichrist begins his reign of terror. And most of them also believe that the rapture will occur at least 3½ years before Antichrist's rule. This belief is based on Daniel 9:24, which says that the seventy weeks relate to the prophet's people (the Jews) and his city (Jerusalem), not to the church.

Some imminent-return Bible teachers, though agreeing that diagram A is probably correct, say that the rapture could conceivably occur at some point during the first half of the seventieth week. They point out that Paul

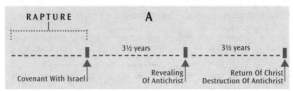

RAPTURE   **A**

3½ years   3½ years

Covenant With Israel   Revealing Of Antichrist   Return Of Christ Destruction Of Antichrist

assures us only that we will be "taken out of the way" before Antichrist reveals his true identity and initiates his program of persecution (2 Th. 2:1-12). They would see the rapture of the church like diagram B.

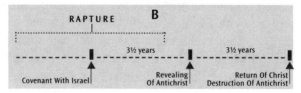

Are You Ready?

Almost 2,000 years have elapsed since two angels told the apostles that Jesus, who had just disappeared behind a cloud, would return in the same way they had seen Him go. Two thousand years is a long time! Generation after generation has looked for His second coming. Unbelievers scoff, and many Christians tend to become complacent. The few who do get excited about Bible prophecy often make blunders that discredit them.

But the prophetic clock keeps ticking. And one of these days, suddenly and unexpectedly, the sound of a heavenly trumpet and a cry of triumph will pierce the air. Then the rapture, the resurrection, and the judgment seat of Christ will occur. But for the unsaved, there will be the revealing of Antichrist, the terrors of the great tribulation, and the devastation of the War of Armageddon.

Are you ready? If you have received Jesus Christ as your Savior, you have no reason to fear an eternal hell.

But if you are living a disobedient life, you will be ashamed and apprehensive when He returns for you.

If you have never acknowledged your sin and placed your trust in Jesus Christ, you will enter the darkest period in all of history. And it's likely that you will become a follower of Antichrist. Second Thessalonians 2:12 tells us that people who heard the truth and rejected it before the rapture of the church are likely to be deluded and destroyed. Receive Jesus Christ as your Savior. And do it today before it's too late!

> "God will send them a strong delusion, that they should believe the lie, that they all may be condemned who did not believe the truth but had pleasure in unrighteousness."
>
> —2 Thessalonians 2:11-12

3

What Can We Know About Daniel's 70 Weeks?

Many of us are skeptical about using numbers or statistics to prove a point. Too many good numbers have been combined with bad assumptions to create misleading conclusions.

But when calculations are carefully handled, they can be an important indicator to resolve controversial issues. We can't afford to ignore the numbers that have the potential to resolve such disputes.

Numbers come into play in the ancient writings of the prophet Daniel. Many believe that in one important prediction Daniel showed us how to calculate the time of Messiah's coming. Did he make such a prediction? And if so, what can we conclude? In the following chapter, RBC senior research editor Herb Vander Lugt surveys the evidence.

MARTIN R. DE HAAN II

The Messiah Question

Many orthodox and conservative Jews believe the time is ripe for the coming of Messiah. They see Israel's return to her homeland after more than 1,900 years of national dispersion as having great prophetic significance. They believe the 1948 rebirth of Israel and waves of immigration from all over the world are converging with many other factors to set the stage for the predicted coming of a national Deliverer. They see the coming of this Messiah as being good not only for Israel but for the whole earth. According to the prophet Isaiah, He will cause the nations to "beat their swords into plowshares, and their spears into pruning hooks; nation shall not lift up sword against nation, neither shall they learn war anymore" (Isa. 2:4).

Many Christians also live with a heightened expectation of the coming of Messiah. They view events occurring in Israel as a likely fulfillment of prophetic Scriptures and have produced a rash of books contending that we are seeing the unprecedented convergence of prophetic indicators. They point out that the increased frequency of natural disasters—floods, tornadoes, hurricanes, earthquakes—are part of the "last days" scenario described in the New Testament.

Messianic hopes are also being fueled by the fear that before long many religious extremists and even criminal organizations like the Mafia will be able to obtain nuclear weapons. The French scholar Jacques Ellul, for example, has said that whether we like it or not, a world dictatorship with a central commerce system to monitor business transactions will be a necessity before long. Without it, nuclear weapons will soon be in the hands of criminals and madmen.

Interestingly, both Jews and Christians share the belief that a period of turmoil and distress will precede the coming of Messiah. The Jewish document called "Talmudic Sages" draws a dark picture of this time. Accordingly, one of these Jewish sages wrote, "Let him [Messiah] come, but let me not see him" (Sanh. 98b). And Christians, though differing quite widely in their view of prophesied endtime events, almost unanimously agree that the rise of an evil world ruler and a time of great tribulation will precede Messiah's return.

> Those who wait for Messiah know that His coming will be preceded by a day of unequaled trouble.

Much of this messianic expectation is rooted in the Old Testament prophecy known as Daniel. No book in the Bible says more about the endtimes than Daniel. Daniel speaks not only of the coming Messiah but of the time of His coming, the marks of His kingdom, and the trouble that will precede it.

Interestingly, the Jews in the Qumran community, which flourished in the first century before Christ and produced the Dead Sea Scrolls, prized Daniel so highly that they may have had more copies of it than any other book. They left eight complete copies and many fragments.

Daniel And His Book. Daniel was among the first of the Jewish hostages who were deported by Nebuchadnezzar, the king of Babylon, in 605 BC. He seems to have been from a prominent family, because he was among the first group of young men selected to receive training for government service in Babylon.

Jews and Christians who take their faiths seriously almost unanimously accept Daniel as the author of the book that bears his name. Even though no other records of Daniel's deportation have been found, the historical setting of the book is well-documented by cuneiform texts. Recognized Old Testament scholars like R. K. Harrison, Gleason Archer, and Leon Wood assure us that everything about the book, including the style of the Hebrew language in which most of it was written and the Aramaic of a few sections, points to sixth-century BC authorship.

But people who do not believe in a personal God and His supernatural involvement in human affairs have a hard time with the idea that it is a sixth-century document. Why? Because in chapters 2 and 7 Daniel presents a foreview of history that took place during the following five centuries—the rise of Medo-Persia, Greece, and Rome as world powers. The 8th chapter describes future developments that correspond to the rise of Greece under Alexander the Great, the division of his empire into four kingdoms after his death, and the activities of Antiochus Epiphanes, a Syrian king who became a notorious enemy of the Jews and their religion during the decade of 160 BC. The 11th chapter also contains a detailed account of unnamed national movements that are now history—the defeat of Medo-Persia by Greece, the partitioning of the Macedonian kingdom into four realms (vv.1-4), the wars between the Ptolemies and Seleucids (vv.5-20), and the great persecution under Antiochus Epiphanes (vv.21-35). All of these events were spelled out in such great detail and match so well what occurred during the fourth, third, and second centuries BC that nonbelievers insist that these sections of the book had to be written during the second century BC.

Anti-supernaturalist critics of Daniel hold their position with great tenacity, because if they don't they must acknowledge Daniel's ability to predict the future. They give the writing of Daniel a late date in spite of a great deal of evidence to the contrary. As mentioned earlier, the language style and content indicate that the book was written by someone living in Babylon during the sixth century BC.

> Anyone who denies the possibility of predictive prophecy must assign a late date to Daniel, in spite of the contrary evidence.

The discovery of excellent manuscript copies among the Dead Sea Scrolls makes it almost mandatory to accept the earlier date for its composition. Why would the Qumran Jews view the book as inspired and make copies of it if they knew it was a contemporary forgery? Two fragments of the book are said by paleographers to be as old as the large Isaiah scroll, which everyone admits was copied several centuries before 160 BC.

Daniel And Messiah. While most of Daniel's prophecies were fulfilled before 150 BC and were related to secular history, some were clearly messianic. He depicted a vision in which he saw the "Ancient of Days" seated in the presence of "ten thousand times ten thousand" in a heavenly court scene (7:9-10). He also saw "One like the Son of Man, coming with the clouds of heaven" to whom the "Ancient of Days" gave "dominion and glory and a kingdom . . . , an everlasting dominion, which shall not pass away" (7:13-14). He depicted "Messiah the Prince," who would appear after a time period of 483 years (9:25-26). He spoke of the "time of the end" when a powerful king would meet his doom, and said that after a time of unprecedented

> Daniel saw "One like the Son of Man," who would come from the heavens to rule the earth.

tribulation God's people would be "delivered," a large company who "sleep in the dust of the earth shall awake," and "those who are wise shall shine . . . like the stars forever and ever" (11:40–12:3).

The coming of someone "like the Son of Man"! A resurrection of bodies! A final judgment! These are magnificent themes that point to the Messiah and His kingdom.

Who is this Messiah and what is His mission? The right answer is a matter of eternal importance. And we believe that it can be found in the Old Testament book of Daniel.

The Prophecy Of Daniel 9

In this study we will focus on the "70 weeks" prophecy of Daniel 9:20-27. We will do so under three headings: (1) Daniel's Portrait of the Messianic Age; (2) Daniel's Messianic Calculations; and (3) Daniel's View of the Endtimes. The analysis of these verses will raise some important questions. If Jesus is the Messiah of Old Testament prophecy, why didn't He usher in the golden age of peace, prosperity, and righteousness predicted by Daniel? How can we know that the "Anointed One" or "Messiah" of verses 25 and 26 is Jesus Christ? What compelling reasons can be given for inserting a long period of time between the end of the 69th week and the beginning of the 70th week? These are valid questions and deserve careful answers.

Daniel's Portrait Of The Messianic Age (Dan. 9:24)

The place was Babylon. The time was 538 BC. And Daniel, who was more than 80 years old, had been reading the book of the prophet Jeremiah. As he read, he dis-covered that God had decreed Israel's time of captivity to last 70 years (Jer. 25:11-12; 29:10).

This discovery impressed Daniel. He longed for the day when the Jewish people could once again possess the city of Jerusalem and worship in their temple. Since he had been taken captive in 605 BC, 67 years had passed. But he wasn't sure that the starting point for the 70 years of judgment was 605 BC. He probably remembered that another group of exiles was deported in 597 BC, and that the final, complete devastation of Jerusalem did not occur until 586 BC. If the 70-year period was reckoned from these dates, the restoration of the Jewish people could be another 20 years away. Troubled by these uncertainties, Daniel began to pray.

While Daniel was still in prayer, the angel Gabriel appeared with a prophecy from God. This message had in view far more than the 70 years of judgment Daniel was concerned about. It would appear to be the master timetable for God's messianic plan.

This prophecy began by predicting that the messianic age would arrive after "70 weeks."

> The angel Gabriel gave Daniel a timetable for the messianic age.

> *Seventy weeks are determined for your people and for your holy city, to finish the transgression, to make an end of sins, to make reconciliation for iniquity, to bring in everlasting righteousness, to seal up vision and prophecy, and to anoint the Most Holy (Dan. 9:24).*

"Seventy weeks" sounds like a relatively short period of time for Daniel to wait. But almost without exception, Jewish and Christian scholars take the "weeks" (lit. "sevens") to represent "sevens" of years. Since a "week" is the translation of a Hebrew word meaning "a seven," most believe that the 70 weeks is a period of 490 years (70 x 7). Some take the number literally. Others, noting that 7 and 70 often have symbolic significance, view the 490 years as an indefinite span of time. In either case, according to the angel Gabriel, the messianic kingdom that will be ushered in at the close of this 70 weeks will be marked by six elements:

1. Transgression Finished. God's 70 weeks will "finish the transgression." The Hebrew word translated *transgression* carries the idea of rebellion against

God. Jews and Christians take this to mean that rebellion against God will end. They also agree that only true believers in God—whether Jew or Gentile—will enter the messianic kingdom. But Christians believe that "to finish the transgression" also includes a national acceptance of Jesus as Messiah.

2. Sin Sealed Up. Daniel also predicted that the 70-week period would "make an end of sins." The word translated *sins* refers to sins other than revolt or rebellion—general immorality, dishonesty, and the like. The verb in the Hebrew text translated "put an end to" in NIV literally means "to seal up." The margin of the Hebrew text uses the word that means "put an end to" or

> The coming of the messianic age will bring an end to both secularism and religious pluralism.

"finish." So most translators have adopted this alternate reading. But the expression "to seal up," the literal rendering of the Hebrew text, should not be lightly dismissed.

R. D. Duncan points out that God "seals up the stars" so they don't shine and that cold weather "seals up the hand" of men so they cannot continue their daily labor (Job 9:7; 37:7). To "seal up" sin is to place people under complete restraint so that among the citizens of the kingdom, sin will be rare by today's standards and judgment for wrongdoing will be administered quickly and justly.

Jews and Christians alike believe that this will occur when Messiah rules the world.

3. *Wickedness Atoned For.* The third accomplishment of God's 70-week program is "to make reconciliation for iniquity" or "to atone for wickedness" (NIV). The verb in this sentence is *kaphar*, the Old Testament term used to denote the covering of sin by making a sacrifice. Hebrew scholar Keil says the form of the verb indicates that the word means "to cover so thoroughly that the sin is obliterated."

Christians see this as having been fulfilled in the death of Jesus Christ, who according to the New Testament gave Himself to die on the cross as the perfect sacrifice. Jewish scholars view the promise of this verse as having to do with reconciliation, but not a reconciliation by a once-for-all sacrifice. They do not accept the idea that Messiah will offer Himself as the final and complete sacrifice. Therefore they take little note of the word *kaphar* as it appears here. They hold that animal sacrifices will be a divine requirement as long as the earth stands. But the words "to make reconciliation for iniquity" seem to denote something unique and special—an atonement that has been accomplished.

4. *Righteousness Established.* The conclusion of the 70-week period will also "bring in everlasting righteousness." This undoubtedly points to the justice and peace of the new social order that Israel has been waiting for since the days of the prophets. It is a mark of the messianic age, which corresponds to what other prophets have also predicted.

> A new world order will occur after the nation of Israel grieves for its sins against God.

According to the prophet Zechariah, it is a coming day of righteousness that will be preceded by a strange mix of national victory and repentance. Zechariah quotes the Lord as saying, "It shall be in that day that I will seek to destroy all the nations that come against Jerusalem. And I will pour on the house of David and on the inhabitants of Jerusalem the Spirit of grace and supplication; then they will look on Me whom they pierced. Yes, they will mourn for Him as one mourns for his only son, and grieve for Him as one grieves for a firstborn" (Zech. 12:9-10).

According to the prophet Ezekiel, the nation will then receive a "new heart" from the One who promised, "I will put My Spirit within you and cause you to walk in My statutes, and you shall keep My judgments, and do them" (Ezek. 36:26-27).

> The messianic age will be the last chapter of God's vision to use one nation to bring blessing to the whole world.

5. Vision And Prophecy Sealed. The fifth element of Daniel's messianic portrait is found in the words "to seal up vision and prophecy." When the messianic age begins, God will, by accomplishing all that was promised through visions and prophecies, stamp His seal on what His servants had spoken. Finally the whole world will understand prophecies that go all the way back to the time God first spoke to Abraham and said, "Get out of your country, from your family and from your father's house, to a land that I will show you. I will make you a great nation; I will bless you and make your name great; and you shall be a blessing. I will bless those who bless you, and I will curse him who curses you; and in you all the families of the earth shall be blessed" (Gen. 12:1-3).

6. The Most Holy Anointed. The sixth achievement of Daniel's messianic portrait involves the anointing of "the Most Holy." Some Jews see this as being fulfilled in the consecration of a rebuilt temple in the days of a yet undisclosed Messiah. Some Christians also believe "the Most Holy" refers to a rebuilt temple. They take literally the temple description of Ezekiel 40–44 and believe that animal sacrifices will once again be offered at the holy place. They believe that this time, however, the sacrifices will be seen as memorials to the One whom John the Baptist called "the Lamb of God who takes away the sin of the world" (Jn. 1:29).

Other Christians, while agreeing that Christ's second coming will usher in this golden age, do not agree that "the Most Holy" refers to a rebuilt temple. They interpret Ezekiel 40–44 as apocalyptic, as teaching spiritual truths through symbols drawn from a familiar form—the temple. They believe Jesus Himself will be anointed as "the Most Holy."

While there is much disagreement among Jewish and Christian communities about how all of this will work out, some things are clear. According to Daniel's portrait, God has a 70-week program that will culminate in an age when spiritual rebellion will end, sin will be restrained, reconciliation will have been accomplished, righteousness will prevail, prophecy will have been fulfilled, and God's anointing of either a new temple and/or His Messiah will occur.

What remains is for us to consider the actual 490-year time period Daniel predicted.

Daniel's Messianic Calculations (Dan. 9:25-26)

After assuring Daniel that at a predetermined time his people and his holy city would experience the full blessings of the messianic age, the angel Gabriel gave  Daniel calculations related to "the Anointed One, the ruler" who is "cut off" so as to "have nothing" (NIV).

> *Know therefore and understand, that from the going forth of the command to restore and build Jerusalem until Messiah the Prince, there shall be seven weeks and sixty-two weeks; the street shall be built again, and the wall, even in troublesome times. And after the sixty-two weeks Messiah shall be cut off, but not for Himself; and the people of the prince who is to come shall destroy the city and the sanctuary. The end of it shall be with a flood, and till the end of the war desolations are determined (Dan. 9:25-26).*

These verses account for 69 of the 70 weeks (lit. "sevens") in God's announced program for Daniel's people and their city.

This prophecy predicts when Messiah will come, that He will die, and that He will die before the destruction of the temple.

This time period begins with "the command to restore and build Jerusalem." The Hebrew word translated "command" in the KJV is *daber*, which literally means "word" and can refer to a "command," a "decree," or a "commission." It depicts an official authorization, in this case to restore and rebuild Jerusalem.

It is necessary to identify the decree in order to know when the "70 weeks" began. It's also necessary to determine what happened "7 weeks" after this time span began, to understand why the "69 weeks" is divided into two segments.

The Pertinent Decree. The Bible records the issuing of three decrees by Gentile kings authorizing the Jews in exile to return to their homeland. The first one was by Cyrus in 539 BC (2 Chr. 36:23; Ezra 1:2-4). But this cannot be the decree Daniel had in mind. It referred only to the temple, making no mention of the city.

The second royal decree involving the Jews and their homeland was made by Artaxerxes in 458 BC (Ezra 7:11-26). Like the decree of Cyrus, no specific mention is made of rebuilding the city of Jerusalem or its walls. However, Ezra must have viewed this decree as authorizing the rebuilding of the city and its walls, because in his prayer of confession recorded in Ezra 9:6-15 he thanked God for giving them the favor of "the kings of Persia, to revive us, to repair the house of our God, to rebuild its ruins, and to give us a wall in Judah and Jerusalem" (v.9).

The third royal decree involving the Jews and their city was issued by the same Artaxerxes in 444 BC (Neh. 2:5-8,17-18). This is specific in authorizing the rebuilding of the city walls.

The 7 Weeks. The text says, "From the going forth of the command . . . . there shall be seven weeks and sixty-two weeks." These 69 weeks culminate in "Messiah the Prince." But why this special mention of 7 weeks? The answer is expressed in the last words of verse 25, "The street shall be built again, and the wall, even in troublesome times." The 7 weeks that precede the 62 weeks is undoubtedly the time period it took for Ezra, Nehemiah, and others to rebuild the city. According to Barnes and several other trustworthy Bible commentators, the historian Prideaux declared that Nehemiah's last action in rebuilding the city occurred in the 15th year of the Persian ruler Darius Nothus (423–404 BC). His 15th year was the 49th year from the 458 BC decree. Josephus seems to support this idea in his remarks about the death of Nehemiah. This is remarkable and can be viewed as an indication that the 458 BC date is correct. But it is possible that some rebuilding continued until 49 years after the 444 BC date.

> The "70 week" time period began with the decree in either 458 BC or in 444 BC.

The 69 Weeks. The 62 weeks plus the 7 weeks brings us to the time of "Messiah the Prince" (v.25), the Messiah who will be "cut off and will have nothing" (v.26 NIV). Christian Bible scholars point out that the period of the first 69 "weeks" (483 years) ends in the days of Jesus of Nazareth, and that either start date of 458 BC or 444 BC is possible.

Both the 458 BC and 444 BC dates have their advocates among Bible scholars. Beginning with 458

BC and using standard chronology, one arrives at AD 26, the year Jesus reached the age of 30 (He was born in 4 BC). It was at the age of 30 that a male descendant of Aaron began his priestly duties.

$$\begin{array}{c} 458 \text{ BC} \\ + \\ \underline{483 \text{ years (365 days each)}} \\ \text{AD 26} \end{array}$$

The text tells us that after 69 weeks (7 + 62) Messiah is "cut off." It doesn't tell us how long after, nor does it indicate that the 70th week would begin as soon as the 69th ended. Bible chronologists generally take either AD 30 or AD 33 as the year of Christ's crucifixion. So adding 483 years to the 458 BC date brings us to the beginning of Jesus' ministry in AD 26 and allows for Him to be "cut off" in AD 30.

$$\begin{array}{c} 444 \text{ BC} \\ + \\ 173{,}880 \text{ days} \\ \text{(483 prophetic years of 360 days} \\ \text{each or 476 solar years} \\ \underline{\text{of 365 days each)}} \\ \text{AD 33} \end{array}$$

The 444 BC decree of Artaxerxes, however, also deserves serious consideration. If one uses "prophetic years" of 360 days each, it is exactly 483 years (173,880 days) from the day of Artaxerxes decree in 444 BC (Neh. 2:1) to the day of Christ's triumphal entry into Jerusalem during the last week of His earthly life (Mt. 21). H. W. Hoehner, a respected biblical scholar, details this in his book *Chronological Aspects Of The Life Of Christ*. It was on that day in AD 33 that Jesus officially announced to the Israelites that He was the Messiah. Later that week He was "cut off" or crucified.

The idea of 360-day prophetic years is taken from the fact that the 1,260 days of Revelation 12:6, the "time and times and half a time" of Revelation 12:14 (3½ years), and the 42 months of Revelation 13:5 are equals—a 3½-year period.

Both of these methods of computing the 483-year time period in relation to Jesus Christ work out in an astounding manner.

The Anointed One. Starting with either 458 BC or 444 BC, the conclusion of the 483 years does indeed coincide remarkably with the date Jesus Christ presented Himself to Israel as her Messiah. But what if this is only an astounding coincidence? A critique of alternative explanations is in order.

Cyrus And Onias. Some scholars (Christian and Jewish) begin the 70 weeks with the decree of Cyrus in 538 BC. But, as mentioned earlier, this decree did not authorize the rebuilding of Jerusalem. Furthermore, this approach requires that the numbers given must be taken symbolically. Taking them literally doesn't tie in with any significant dates in the history of Israel.

Other scholars see two "messiahs" in the prophecy and make Cyrus the Great the first "anointed one." They point out that at the time of Jerusalem's complete desolation (587 BC), God assured Jeremiah that the city would be rebuilt (Jer. 29:10). From this authoritative word until Cyrus in 538 BC was indeed 49 years or 7 "weeks." But to make this interpretation work, they must rearrange the Hebrew word order and translate Daniel 9:25-26 as follows:

> Know therefore and understand: From the time that the word went out to restore and rebuild

Jerusalem [God's word expressed in Jeremiah 29:10 in 587 BC] until the time of an anointed prince, there shall be 7 weeks; and for 62 weeks it shall be built with streets and moat, but in troubled times. And after the 62 weeks, an anointed one shall be cut off, and shall have nothing.

Most of these scholars view the second "anointed one" as Onias, the legitimate high priest who was murdered in 171 BC without a successor. But the second cluster of 62 weeks from 538 BC to 171 BC is 367 years, not the 434 years Daniel predicted. Moreover, as noted earlier, the translation given by these scholars is possible only if one alters the word order of the Hebrew text and makes a few changes dictated by opinion, not by the rules of grammar. One should explore all the possibilities of coming up with a workable interpretation of a text as it stands before altering or modifying it.

> One should explore all the possibilities of coming up with a workable interpretation of a text as it stands before altering or modifying it.

Cyrus And Phananias. Some current Jewish scholars translate Daniel 9:25-26 essentially the same as the Revised Version translators did. They view the 70 weeks as beginning with God's decree announced in Jeremiah 29:10 in 587 BC and take Cyrus to be the first anointed prince. They see "the Anointed One [who] will be cut off and will have nothing" (NIV) as the priesthood of AD 70. To make Daniel's numbers work out, the advocates of this interpretation use a dating system that brings the 490-year period ("70 weeks") to the time Jerusalem was destroyed by the Romans. They say the destruction of the temple in AD 70 has ushered in the age of Messiah. From this point on, they say, Israel had no hope but in the Messiah whom God will send to fulfill all the messianic elements Daniel described.

This viewpoint, however, raises even more problems than those considered earlier. The time span from 587 BC to AD 70 is 658 years, not 490. Furthermore, it is difficult to think of either the priesthood or the high priest of AD 70 as being God's anointed. The last high priest was Phananias who was appointed to this position by a group of zealots after they had killed the Roman appointee Ananias. And the high priesthood during the first century was an office manipulated by the Sadducees and Romans to keep the Jewish people under control. Old Testament qualifications were not even considered. The high priests certainly were not God's appointees.

Jesus Christ. Reading the Hebrew text as it stands and beginning the 483 years of Daniel 9:25-26 with a well-documented royal decree in either 458 BC or 444 BC results in the conclusion that Daniel's 69 "weeks" ends with the date of Christ's presentation of Himself as Messiah.

Moreover, the declaration that this Messiah will be "cut off and will have nothing" (NIV) needs no manipulation to be seen as a declaration of His crucifixion. The Hebrew word translated "cut off" refers to the execution of wrongdoers (Lev. 7:20; Ps. 37:9; Prov.

2:22). Christians believe this is most appropriate because, according to the New Testament, God made Christ "to be sin for us" (2 Cor. 5:21). Although He had never sinned, He died as a wrongdoer to pay the price for our sin. Even the method of His death (crucifixion) was that of a criminal.

> The most logical conclusion is that Daniel's 69 "weeks" ends with the date of Christ's presentation of Himself as Messiah.

Christians believe the expression "will have nothing" is an accurate representation of the fact that Jesus died without apparent followers or possessions. It seemed to onlookers that He was a dismal failure.

The Messianic Age. But there is a problem. Even those who believe everything the New Testament says about Jesus Christ's birth, death, and resurrection must admit that Jesus' coming did not usher in all the blessings listed in Daniel 9:24. He did not "finish the transgression," "make an end of sins," "bring in everlasting righteousness," "seal up vision and prophecy," or "anoint the Most Holy."

All that can be argued is that He did "make reconciliation for iniquity" by His sacrificial death. (As noted earlier, the Hebrew text carries the thought of making atonement.) By doing this, Christians believe, He put an end to the sacrificial system of the Old Testament. This concept is stated repeatedly in the New Testament books of Galatians and Hebrews. The message "Believe on the Lord Jesus Christ, and you will be saved" (Acts 16:31) is offered repeatedly to all people everywhere. In that sense, Christians believe the messianic age has begun. When the Holy Spirit, accompanied by a sound of rushing wind and fiery tongues, descended upon a group of believers 10 days after Christ ascended, the apostle Peter told the crowd that had gathered:

> *This is what was spoken by the prophet Joel: "And it shall come to pass in the last days, says God, that I will pour out of My Spirit on all flesh; your sons and your daughters shall prophesy, your young men shall see visions, your old men shall dream dreams. And on My menservants and on My maidservants I will pour out My Spirit in those days; and they shall prophesy. I will show wonders in heaven above and signs in the earth beneath: blood and fire and vapor of smoke. The sun shall be turned into darkness, and the moon into blood, before the coming of the great and awesome day of the Lord. And it shall come to pass that whoever calls on the name of the Lord shall be saved"* (Acts 2:16-21).

Some elements in Joel's prophecy (Joel 2:28-32) were not fulfilled on the Day of Pentecost. But, according to Peter, the age of the Spirit had arrived—the age that would culminate in the celestial disturbances accompanying the second coming of Jesus Christ. Similarly, Christians from the beginning have believed that the death, burial, and resurrection of Jesus Christ paid the price for sin, broke the power of death (1 Cor. 15), defeated Satan (Heb. 2:14-15), and ushered in a new age.

When will the full realization of that which Daniel predicted occur?

When will the full realization of that which Daniel predicted occur? Christians believe it will happen when Israel turns to Jesus Christ as Messiah. Remember, Daniel 9:24 opens with the words, "Seventy weeks are determined for *your* people and *your* holy city." The 69th week has ended, but the last week has not yet begun. It is after 70 weeks that the fullness of the blessings will come.

Daniel's View Of The Endtimes (Dan. 9:26-27)

 From a New Testament point of view, the term "last days" takes in the entire time period from the apostles to Christ's second coming. From this perspective, everything in Daniel 9:26-27 that followed Messiah being "cut off" is part of the endtimes. In these verses, Daniel first described what happens after the 69th week ends but before the 70th week begins. Then he depicted the events of this 70th week.

The Destruction Of Jerusalem In AD 70. After "Messiah the Prince" is "cut off," the people of a coming prince will destroy Jerusalem.

> *After the sixty-two weeks Messiah shall be cut off, but not for Himself; and the people of the prince who is to come shall destroy the city and the sanctuary. The end of it shall be with a flood, and till the end of the war desolations are determined (Dan. 9:26).*

A new hostile prince comes into the picture. He is

literally "a prince, the one coming." The use of the article in "the one coming" suggests that this coming prince has been introduced earlier. He is undoubtedly the "little horn" of Daniel 7:8,24-26 who makes war with the saints until the Ancient of Days intervenes. He will head the restored Roman Empire in the endtimes.

His "people," the Romans, destroyed Jerusalem in AD 70. These words in Daniel 9:26 cannot refer to Antiochus Epiphanes of the second century BC, because he destroyed neither the city of Jerusalem nor the temple.

The phrase "the end will come like a flood" (NIV) perhaps points to both the destruction of Jerusalem in AD 70 and the end of the age. It will come suddenly and overwhelmingly. Until that end comes, wars will mark human history. And "desolation," especially in relation to Daniel's people and his city, will continue.

What desolation? Eric Sauer points out that 1.1 million Jews were killed in AD 70; 500,000 killed in AD 132-134; 1,200 killed in Rhineland, Germany, in AD 1096; 100,000 killed in Bavaria and Austria in AD 1298; 400,000 killed during the Russian-Polish-Swedish war in 1648-1658; and 4 to 6 million killed in Nazi Germany between 1935 and 1945. And no one knows how much suffering lies ahead for the people the prophet Zechariah called "the apple of His eye" (2:8).

The Antichrist In The 70th Week. The 70th week will begin when someone with authority will make a binding commitment with a group of people called "the many." After 3½ years he will break his agreement. This will be accompanied by some kind of sacrilege. But in

the end, the person who breaks the treaty and engages
in this abomination will meet his doom.

> *Then he shall confirm a covenant with many for one*
> *week; but in the middle of the week he shall bring an*
> *end to sacrifice and offering. And on the wing of*
> *abominations shall be one who makes desolate, even*
> *until the consummation, which is determined, is*
> *poured out on the desolate (Dan. 9:27).*

It seems obvious that this 70th week does not
immediately follow the 69th week. The time period
of 7 weeks plus 62 weeks
extends from the decree to **It seems obvious that the**
restore Jerusalem *to* "Mes- **70th week does not immedi-**
siah the Prince" (v.25). It is **ately follow the 69th week.**
after this time period of 49
years plus 434 years that the Messiah is "cut off," and
the city and sanctuary are destroyed. No time spans
are given for these events, which are both well-attested
historically. Moreover, to view verse 27 as taking us
back to the Messiah who was "cut off" doesn't work
out very well. Jesus did not make a covenant. And He
wasn't the kind of man who would make a 7-year
covenant and then break it.

Since the events described in verse 27 cannot be
tied in with the time of Christ's crucifixion, the
destruction of Jerusalem, or anything that happened in
the first century, the text must look to the future.

The man who "shall confirm a covenant with many
for one week" is undoubtedly the ruler introduced to us
in verse 26 as "the prince who is to come." As noted
earlier, he is the "little horn" of Daniel 7. He will head

a western confederacy of nations, the revived Roman Empire in its "ten toes" phase of Daniel 2:40-43, the "ten horned" phase of Daniel 7:24. This same individual is referred to as the "man of sin" (2 Th. 2:3), the "Antichrist" (1 Jn. 2:18), and the "beast" (Rev. 13:1-10). He will apparently pose as a friend of Israel, giving the Jewish people a sense of security and allowing them to worship in their newly rebuilt temple. Revelation 13 opens with this man receiving the adulation of all mankind. He will have unified the Western world. He will have brought order out of chaos. People will feel confidence in his goodness. It is then that he dares to drop all pretense and show himself to be Satan's henchman. He begins to blaspheme God and "make war with the saints and to overcome them" (vv.6-7). From this point on, he remains in power for 42 months before meeting his doom.

The final statement of Daniel 9:27 is difficult to translate, but the rendering in the NIV clarifies the meaning. He will "set up an abomination that causes desolation." Three New Testament passages throw some light on these words: Matthew 24:15, 2 Thessalonians 2:3-4, and Revelation 13.

Addressing Jewish people, Jesus said, "Therefore when you see the abomination of desolation, spoken of by Daniel the prophet, standing in the holy place, . . . then let those who are in Judea flee" (Mt. 24:15). It appears that the image of Antichrist will be placed in the temple and that people will be ordered to worship it. This is the abominable event that will trigger the desolation of the temple and the city of Jerusalem at the end of the age.

Paul, instructing Christian believers about the coming time of tribulation that will precede Christ's return to set up His kingdom, declared that during this period of trouble the "man of sin" will be revealed, describing him as one "who opposes and exalts himself above all that is called God and that is

> "He shall exalt and magnify himself above every god."
> —Daniel 11:36

worshiped, so that he sits as God in the temple of God, showing himself that he is God" (2 Th. 2:3-4).

Revelation 13 tells us that he will start a war against the saints and blaspheme God. Then his partner, the False Prophet, will make an image of the Beast (Antichrist) and demand that people worship it or die. Jesus and Paul both indicated that this outrageous blasphemy will take place in the restored Jewish temple. The devil himself as the Antifather (the dragon of Rev. 13:4), the Antichrist (the Beast), and the Antispirit (the False Prophet) are the infernal trinity. They will attempt to make the restored Jewish temple their religious headquarters, the place where they will be worshiped.

The last words of Daniel 9:27, "until the end that is decreed is poured out on him" (NIV), indicate Antichrist's doom. Other Scriptures clearly declare that he will be totally and disgracefully defeated. His final series of battles and his destruction are portrayed in Daniel 11:40-45. This passage closes with the words, "Yet he shall come to his end, and no one will help him."

Israel's Conversion In The 70th Week. Daniel 9 closes, as noted above, with a summary statement about the shocking sacrilege and predetermined doom of the future world ruler the Bible calls the Beast, the man of sin, and the Antichrist. His defeat is further described in Daniel 11:40-45. But that's not the end of the story. Daniel 12:1-3 gives a summary of what will happen to the Israelites as a nation:

> *At that time Michael shall stand up, the great prince who stands watch over the sons of your people; and there shall be a time of trouble, such as never was since there was a nation, even to that time. And at that time your people shall be delivered, every one who is found written in the book. And many of those who sleep in the dust of the earth shall awake, some to everlasting life, some to shame and everlasting contempt. Those who are wise shall shine like the brightness of the firmament, and those who turn many to righteousness like the stars forever and ever (Dan. 12:1-3).*

"At that time" refers to the interval between the rise of Antichrist and his destruction. During this time of great tribulation—tribulation for Israel predicted in Deuteronomy 4:30, Jeremiah 30:7, Matthew 24:21-22, and many other Bible passages—the archangel Michael will see to it that the Israelites are not annihilated. Multitudes of Jewish people will repent and believe in their Messiah. Zechariah 12 graphically depicts God's supernatural deliverance of the surviving Israelites at the close of this terrible time. He then describes the repentant nation as Messiah returns to establish His kingdom:

> *I will pour on the house of David and on the inhabitants of Jerusalem the Spirit of grace and supplica-*

tion; then they will look on Me whom they pierced. Yes, they will mourn for Him as one mourns for his only son, and grieve for Him as one grieves for a first-born (Zech. 12:10).

The Jewish people who still refuse to believe will be removed in judgment (Ezek. 20:33-38). Therefore, all the Israelites who go into the full blessings of the kingdom age will be true believers, people whose names appear in the book of life. All the promises in Daniel 9:24 will be realized. The prophet Isaiah portrays what will then occur:

Now it shall come to pass in the latter days that the mountain of the Lord's house shall be established on the top of the mountains, and shall be exalted above the hills; and all nations shall flow to it. Many people shall come and say, "Come, and let us go up to the mountain of the Lord, to the house of the God of Jacob; He will teach us His ways, and we shall walk in His paths." For out of Zion shall go forth the law, and the word of the Lord from Jerusalem. He shall judge between the nations, and rebuke many people; they shall beat their swords into plowshares, and their spears into pruning hooks; nation shall not lift up sword against nation, neither shall they learn war anymore (Isa. 2:2-4).

And what about the Israelites whose bodies have turned to dust? They will not be forgotten! The Christian scholar Tregelles, following earlier Jewish commentators, translated verse 2, "And many from the sleepers of the dust of the earth shall awake, these shall be to everlasting life; but those of the rest of the sleepers, those who do not awake at this time, shall be unto shame and everlasting contempt." The coming of God's Messiah will be a tremendous event for all the believing Israelites of all the ages!

What Do We Believe?

Are we at a crisis point in human history? Many conservative Jews and Christians believe we are. They see as highly significant the fact that Israel is often at the center of world news with her internal conflicts and her treaties with Arab neighbors. They insist that we are inevitably moving toward such internationalization that mankind is ripe for a world dictator who could easily be the Antichrist.

On the other hand, some Christians believe we are on the verge of a worldwide spiritual revival. People are becoming alarmed at world conditions. Reports of spiritual awakenings in India, Africa, and countries in Central and South America support this optimistic outlook.

We believe the next event in God's prophetic program is described by the apostle Paul:

> *The Lord Himself will descend from heaven with a shout, with the voice of an archangel, and with the trumpet of God. And the dead in Christ will rise first. Then we who are alive and remain shall be caught up together with them in the clouds to meet the Lord in the air. And thus we shall always be with the Lord (1 Th. 4:16-17).*

The Scriptures indicate that this "catching up," or rapture, of those who are "in Christ" must take place before Antichrist reveals his true identity.

Paul wrote his letter to the Thessalonians in part because some of them thought they had entered the great tribulation of the endtimes. Paul assured them that they were wrong and said it would not begin until after the man of sin had been revealed (2 Th. 2:1-3). He went on to explain:

> *Now you know what is restraining, that he may be revealed in his own time. For the mystery of lawlessness is already at work; only He who now restrains will do so until He is taken out of the way (2 Th. 2:6-7).*

It's important that we see the Holy Spirit and the church together as the *restrainer* mentioned in this text. The third-person masculine pronoun suggests the Holy Spirit. As God, He is always present everywhere. He cannot be "taken out of the way." But He can leave the earth as the *restrainer* when the Lord catches up His church to be with Himself. His departure in this sense will open the door for Antichrist to make his move.

This identification of the restrainer fits the context of 2 Thessalonians 2 better than any other suggested interpretation. Good reasons can be given for rejecting the idea that the restrainer who will be removed is the devil, an angel, or civil government. This passage of Scripture gives us solid reasons for believing that the return of Christ for His church could occur at any moment.

Believers therefore must live in healthy tension. On the one hand, we are looking for His any-moment coming for us. On the other hand, because we do not know exactly where we are in God's endtime program, we pray and work to spread the good news about Jesus Christ. The fact that the nation of Israel is making treaties reminds us of Bible passages about the endtimes. It heightens our sense of anticipation. The news about multitudes turning to Christ throughout the world moves us to pray and give and work.

> The Bible has a solemn warning to those who have heard the gospel and have not believed.

For nonbelievers, the fact that Christ could return at any moment has ominous overtones. The Bible has a solemn warning to those who have heard the gospel and have not believed. Paul declared that when the Antichrist is revealed, it may be too late for a change of mind:

> *The coming of the lawless one is according to the working of Satan, with all power, signs, and lying wonders, and with all unrighteous deception among those who perish, because they did not receive the love of the truth, that they might be saved. And for this reason God will send them strong delusion, that they should believe the lie, that they all may be condemned who did not believe the truth but had pleasure in unrighteousness (2 Th. 2:9-12).*

Now is the time to make the decision to trust Jesus as Messiah. Tomorrow may be too late. "Behold, now is the accepted time; behold, now is the day of salvation" (2 Cor. 6:2).

4

What Can We Know About The Second Coming?

Where do we stand after 2,000 years of false alarms and the current "future fatigue"? Should we join those who have thrown in the towel on prophetic study in favor of "more practical, life-related issues"? Or, if we are convinced that nothing is more practical than to look for our Lord's return, how should we do that? Should we be expecting an any-moment return? Or should we be more concerned about preparing for the coming years of unparalleled trouble that the prophets predicted?

In an effort to answer some of these questions, Herb Vander Lugt and Dave Branon have written this chapter. It is our prayer that their work will lead you to an increased awareness of what the Bible has to say about our Lord's promised return.

MARTIN R. DE HAAN II

Christians Divided On
The Rapture Question

MILLIONS REPORTED MISSING
News reports arriving from cities around the globe tell of a mysterious disappearance of thousands and thousands of people. In some instances entire families have vanished without a trace . . . .

Could this headline and lead paragraph appear in your newspaper tomorrow? Is it possible that Christ could return today and suddenly remove His children from this earth, leaving an unbelieving world to wonder where all the Christians have gone?

This is an extremely practical issue. If Christ could return today, we need to be ready. We cannot afford to take the future for granted. Just as a child finds the inner strength to pull his act together when he thinks his dad is coming through the front door, so those who live in the expectation that Christ could return at any moment have reason to live a different and better life. It gives husbands reason to love their wives and to spend time with their children. It gives managers incentive to be considerate of their workers and to treat them the way they would want to be treated. It gives everyone who knows the way to heaven urgent reason to introduce others to Christ—before it is too late.

But, having said that, could Christ return today? Church people do not all agree. While all true Christians believe in the return of Christ, many disagree about the details of when it will occur.

Some think that Christ will come back at the end of the age just prior to destroying and recreating the heavens and the earth. This is termed *amillennialism* because it does not recognize a literal millennium (1,000-year reign of Christ on earth).

Others believe that Christ will return only after a predicted period of unparalleled trouble. This view is called *posttribulationalism* because it sees Christ coming for His people after the tribulation.

> The return of Christ represents not only the ultimate sense of accountability but the ultimate sense of hope as well.

Still others, however, believe that our Lord will return in two phases—once for the salvation of His church and once for the rescue of the nation of Israel. This view includes those who hold to either a *pretribulational* or a *midtribulational* approach to the Lord's return.

But with these options before us, what do we really know about the second coming of Christ? To begin, we know that everyone who looks for Christ's return has reason to live the kind of life that will please the Lord at His coming. The apostle John recognized this when he wrote, "When He is revealed, we shall be like Him, for we shall see Him as He is. And everyone who has this hope in Him purifies himself, just as He is pure" (1 Jn. 3:2-3).

Beyond that incentive for right living, we believe it is very important for us to be ready for a two-part return of Christ, the first phase of which could occur at any moment—maybe even today.

But what is the evidence for such a position?

Why Would Christ Return Again . . . And Again?

The main evidence for a two-part return of Christ revolves around (1) God's distinct plans for Israel and the church and (2) prophecies that describe the time of Christ's return as being both knowable and unknowable. The reasoning might seem to be a little involved at points, but the main point to keep in mind is that Scripture teaches us to be always ready for the Lord's return. The following pages will explain why that seems to signal a two-part return of Christ—one for the church and one for Israel.

The Distinction Between Israel And The Church

Basic to this discussion is our belief that the first of these two returns is for the rescue and removal of the church (1 Cor. 15:51-53; 1 Th. 4:13-18; 5:9). The second relates to God's plan for Israel (Ezek. 36:16-38; Jer. 23:5-6; Rev. 19:11-21). Both have different places in God's prophetic program. Even though both share a common spiritual ancestry that can be traced back to the faith of Abraham (Gal. 3:7), they have different places in God's world plan. Israel represents a nation with whom God has made very earth-centered and geographically related promises (Isa. 2:1-6; Ezek. 36–37). But the church is a multinational organism made up of all true believers in Christ—Jew or Gentile. The church is at the center of God's program until "the fullness of the Gentiles" is fulfilled (Rom. 11:25) and has been given a hope that is to be realized more in heaven than on earth (1 Th. 4:13-18).

The distinction between Israel and the church is basic to understanding prophecy. Many have called it the key to unlocking what the Bible says about the future. When the two are kept distinct, many prophetic details fall into place. Then it becomes evi-

A two-phase return would explain why Israel but not the church is mentioned in the endtime events of Revelation.

dent that some predictions refer to the Lord's return for the church, while others relate to His return as the King and Deliverer of Israel.

This provides an explanation for why the church is not specifically referred to in most of the book of Revelation. Revelation 6–18 (which describes the "great tribulation" to which Jesus alluded in Matthew 24:15-28) never mentions the church. While an argument from silence is not the strongest, it does seem significant. It gives credence to the idea that Christ will have returned to remove the church prior to all of those endtime events related to the restoration and salvation of the nation of Israel, called the "time of Jacob's trouble" (Jer. 30:7). The church will already be with her Lord and will come with Him when He returns to save Israel and set up His promised earthly kingdom.

That brings us to a second important reason for being ready for a two-part return of Christ. The teaching of the Bible includes (a) prophecies of dramatic events that will occur just prior to the Lord's second coming to earth and (b) predictions of another coming at a time that is not expected. It seems reasonable to resolve this apparent contradiction by seeing them as describing two different phases of the Lord's return.

> A two-phase return makes sense if the first phase (for the church) could happen at any time and the second phase (for Israel) happens at a definite, presignaled time.

Just keep in mind that if this discussion seems unrelated to your real needs and problems, you're missing something. Nothing is more practical than the return of Christ. When seen properly, nothing provides more hope. Nothing provides more accountability. Nothing puts the pains and pleasures of life in better perspective than the promise of our Lord's return.

If the Lord were to return today, all of your worst problems and all of your deepest pleasures would suddenly look entirely different. For that reason, let's take a closer look at what the Bible has to say about (1) the any-moment return for the church and (2) the final presignaled event climaxing the worst trouble the world has ever seen.

The Distinction Between An Any-Moment And A Presignaled Return

In the Olivet Discourse, delivered only shortly before His crucifixion, Jesus answered questions raised by His disciples after He had predicted the destruction of the temple at Jerusalem. They asked, "Tell us, when will these things be? And what will be the sign of Your coming, and of the end of the age?" (Mt. 24:3).

Notice that the disciples' question has three parts: (1) When? (2) What will be the signs of Christ's coming? (3) What will be the signs of the end of the age? As we read our Lord's answer, we find that He began with the sign part of the question. He dealt with the signs of His coming that will alert all generations (vv.3-14), the signs of the end of the age related to Israel (vv.15-35), and the "when" or time question related to His unannounced coming for the church (vv.36-51).

The Signs Of His Coming—Alerting All Generations (vv.3-14). The Lord began by describing seven events that would occur before His return. They will be signs of His coming because their purpose will be to remind His children throughout the age, saying, "Jesus is coming again." Our Lord talked about false christs (v.5), wars and rumors of wars (v.6), famines (v.7), pestilences and earthquakes (v.7), persecution (v.9), defections from the faith (vv.10-13), and worldwide preaching of the gospel (v.14).

It is a fact of history that all seven of these occurrences took place to some degree during the first century. However, like most prophecies, the near-at-hand and far-off elements were blended together into one picture. Therefore, Jesus' statements have different applications to different generations. To believers who lived and died under terrible persecution, "the end" in verse 13 is the end of life. But to those who live during the coming tribulation, it will be the end of the age. Similarly, the worldwide preaching of the gospel during the first century was to the Roman world (Col. 1:5-6), while for us today it is to the entire globe.

These events portrayed by our Lord served as signs to first-century believers and to those of all subsequent generations that He is coming again.

The Signs Of The End Of The Age—Related To Israel (vv.15-35). At verse 15, we suddenly find ourselves with a very specific prediction about "an abomination of desolation." This is followed by a detailed description of a brief, terrible time of trouble that will end when the Lord returns. We might be puzzled by the statement about the "abomination of desolation" in the "holy place." But the Jewish people to whom Jesus spoke understood it. They knew that according to Daniel 9:24-27 a hostile Gentile ruler would someday desecrate their temple and initiate horrendous persecution. While Luke 21:20-24 contains some elements that were partially fulfilled in the destruction of Jerusalem and the temple in AD 70, Matthew 24:15-31 focuses on the endtime. There will be:

- Enough fear to drive the Jews to the hills (vv.16-18).
- Unparalleled trouble and woe (vv.19-20).
- Great tribulation that would threaten all life if the days were not shortened (vv.21-22).
- False christs and prophets (vv.23-26).
- Startling celestial signs and the visible descent of the Son of Man "with power and great glory" (vv.29-31).

These will be the signs that the end of the age is near. Just as the appearing of buds on trees signals the soon onset of the summer season, so do these signs show "that it is near, at the very doors" (v.33). In fact, the generation that sees the beginning of these signs (the desecration of the Jewish temple depicted in verse 15) will not pass off the scene before the Lord has returned (v.34).

The "When" Question—Related To His Unan-nounced Return For The Church (vv.36-51). After reminding His disciples that people who see the signs He had spoken of can be sure that the return will be near, Jesus began to answer the "when" question. He didn't set a date. He said His second coming would catch people by surprise (see Lk. 12:40).

First, Jesus explained that the coming of the Son of Man would be "as the days of Noah were." In those days, despite Noah's warnings of danger, the people went about their lives as usual. There was no concern for an imminent flood, because the people didn't believe it was com-

> How can the Lord's second coming catch people by surprise if it's going to be presignaled by all the spectacular events described in Matthew 24?

ing. There were no heavenly signs or unusual events— only the incessant hammering and sawing by Noah and his sons. When the rains came, the people were caught by surprise.

After giving a couple of examples of what will happen when His unexpected coming takes place, our Lord makes this sobering, yet exciting warning:

Therefore you also be ready, for the Son of Man is coming at an hour you do not expect (Mt. 24:44).

How can the Lord's second coming catch people by surprise if it is going to be presignaled by all the striking and spectacular events described in Matthew 24:15-31? That's a key question. The best answer seems to be found in seeing the Lord's second coming as occurring in two stages. First He will come to catch up (or "rapture") His own people. This event will be unannounced. Then He will return to establish His kingdom over the earth. This event will be clearly presignaled.

Matthew 24 describes both stages of Jesus' return: the surprise, any-moment rapture of believers (vv.36-44) and the glorious return of Jesus at the close of the tribulation to end the destruction and establish His kingdom (vv.15-35). He began with the glorious return because that was the concern of the disciples when they asked the question. He introduced the unexpected element to prepare them for the truths about the church age and rapture—truths that would be made clear after His ascension.

> Why didn't the Lord spell out the details of His second coming so clearly that we could put them together and know exactly how and when it will occur?

Purposeful Ambiguity

If you have read our Lord's prophetic words recorded in Matthew 24, Mark 13, and Luke 17 and 21, you probably wish you could find somebody who would give you a crystal-clear explanation of all He said. If so, join the club! Many people have had the same experience and asked, "Why didn't He spell out the details of His second coming so clearly that we could put them together and know exactly how and when it will occur?" The answer is quite simple: He didn't set out to give us this kind of information. His aim was to teach us that we should live in continual readiness for our meeting with Him.

In blending together into one picture references to the destruction of Jerusalem in AD 70, the endtime sacrilege in the temple, the apostolic persecution, the endtime great tribulation, the signs in the heavenly bodies, and an unexpected coming, the Lord followed the pattern of the Old Testament prophets. In their prophecies they also merged, without explanation about sequence, predictions that would occur at four different time periods: (1) in their own lifetime, (2) in the near future, (3) at Messiah's first coming, and (4) at the end of time. For example, the prophecies of Jesus' birth, exaltation, rule, suffering, and death (Isa. 7:14; 52:13–54:17; Jer. 23:5; Mic. 5:4) were written in such a way that they could not be placed in chronological order until they were fulfilled.

We can be thankful that God doesn't tell each of us individually the exact time or manner of our death. Similarly, He didn't give us a precise answer to the what, when, and how questions regarding our Lord's return. It's better for us to live in the tension produced by the realization, "Perhaps today, but maybe not in my lifetime."

Imminency Parables

At the conclusion of the Olivet Discourse, Jesus told two parables that shout out the message, "Be ready!"

In the first one (Mt. 24:45-51), the servant is left in charge while his master is away on a trip. He begins thinking that the owner will be gone a long time, so he abuses the people under him and lives it up. But the master returns unexpectedly and punishes him severely.

In the second parable (Mt. 25:1-13), 10 virgins are invited to attend a wedding reception, but they have to wait for the arrival of the wedding procession. They know it is coming, but they don't know just when. The procession in which each person carries a lighted torch arrives, but five of the girls can't join the group because they have no oil in their torches. However, the five who are prepared become part of the rejoicing company. The message is clear. "We don't know when Jesus is coming back. Therefore, be ready!"

Down through the centuries Bible expositors have applied these parables to the church. The servant who behaved wickedly and the five girls who had no oil represent professing Christians who are not truly saved. When Jesus comes unexpectedly for His own, He will punish them and exclude them from His banquet hall. What a call to readiness! What a powerful intimation of imminency!

Some Don't Agree

When the Lord appears in the air unexpectedly to take His people to heaven, many Christians will be just as surprised as non-Christians. That is because many believers are not convinced that the rapture of the church could occur at any moment. They know that Jesus is coming back, but they do not see His return in two stages. They don't keep an eye on the sky. Let's look at their objections to an imminent rapture.

OBJECTION: The Any-Moment Rapture Is A Recent Idea In Church History. A common objection to the any-moment, pretribulational doctrine of Christ's return relates to its supposed recent origin. Some posttribulationists attempt to show that it began in the 1820s with an unstable Scottish clergyman named Edward Irving. They say that he was the first person to develop the idea that Christ's return would occur in two stages, and that an eccentric named Margaret Macdonald picked up on his teaching during the 1830s. Then, a few years later, J. N. Darby and several other Plymouth Brethren teachers further developed the idea of the two-stage return. Posttribulationists tell us to reject the any-moment rapture idea because it, like the teachings of the Mormons and Jehovah's Witnesses, is of recent and dubious origin.

Before we obey these critics and bid farewell to our belief in the rapture, let's think through their charge. Was the any-moment teaching really new? Did the two-stage teaching originate with evil, irresponsible people as posttribulationists claim? Did the teaching of the second coming develop differently from other important doctrines? We'll find that each of the above questions can be given a solid answer of no.

1. The any-moment idea was not new. The writings of the church fathers are filled with warnings to live in continual readiness for our Lord's return. These men applied the parable of Jesus about the wise and foolish virgins to the people of their age, urging them to keep their lamps burning so they would be ready for Jesus at His return for them. They probably didn't see the need to develop a concept of two stages in the Lord's return because they tended to identify the Antichrist with the Roman Empire and sometimes thought of themselves as already in the great tribulation.

Christians down through the centuries, mindful of the warning of Jesus that His coming would catch the world by surprise, never felt comfortable saying that Jesus Christ could not come at any moment. Many Christians expected Christ's return during great natural disasters like earthquakes or tornadoes. When the dust storms during the early 1930s caused an eerie daytime darkness in some of our midwestern states, many Christians panicked, thinking that the second coming was at hand.

The idea that the Lord could come at any moment certainly did not originate with Edward Irving. In fact, it didn't even originate with Darby. He simply tried to develop a biblical viewpoint that would explain how the imminent-return idea could be harmonized with the teaching of the Bible about a tribulation *prior* to the return.

2. The Plymouth Brethren who developed the two-stage teaching were biblical scholars. The claim that Irving and Macdonald clearly taught the two-stage second coming doctrine rests on flimsy evidence. In fact, their writings on this subject are confusing. While Darby and his Plymouth Brethren associates may have picked up some ideas from Irving and Macdonald, they developed their teaching through a careful and systematic study of the Scriptures in the original languages. They were systematic in the application of the Scriptures. They rejected some elements of Irving's teachings and produced a sane and coherent doctrine of last things. These men, like Augustine, Luther, Calvin, and Wesley, had flaws and blind spots. But like them, they were also sincere men of God who made tremendous contributions to the church in both leadership and doctrine.

3. The method of development for this two-stage return idea is similar to that of other doctrines. The doctrines of justification, sanctification, and God's sovereignty, though taught by Christian leaders down through the centuries, were never as fully developed as they were by Luther, Calvin, and Wesley. Throughout the years of church history, the Holy Spirit has led the Lord's people into clearer understanding of God's Word in every area of Christian doctrine, including that of the second coming.

In summary, the claim that we should abandon the pretribulation, any-moment doctrine of Christ's return because of a recent and dubious origin carries no weight. The logic that rejects a teaching on this basis demands that we also reject Luther's teaching on justification, Calvin's insights into God's sovereignty, and Wesley's contributions toward an understanding of sanctification.

OBJECTION: The Rapture Is Not In Scripture. If we are to consider ourselves people who "go by the Book," we have to be careful that we never support an argument by adding to the Bible something that isn't there. One of those "somethings" that isn't found in God's Word is the word *rapture.*

When we use this word to designate the time of Jesus' return in the air to take His followers to heaven, though, we are not violating Scripture. For example, the word *Trinity* doesn't appear in the Bible, but posttribulationists don't deny its truth.

Where, then, does the term *rapture* come from? In 1 Thessalonians 4:17, Paul said that living believers will be "caught up" with the dead in Christ to meet the Lord in the air. The Greek word Paul used here is *harpazo*, which means "to snatch away." When the Bible was translated into Latin, the scholars rendered *harpazo* as *rapturo*. It is just a short step then from *rapturo*

> The claim that we should abandon the pretribulation, any-moment doctrine of Christ's return because of a recent and dubious origin carries no weight.

to the English word *rapture*. Therefore, although it is true that the word itself does not appear in our English translation of Scripture, the sense of the word is surely there. Christians will be snatched away when the Lord descends with a shout.

OBJECTION: Jesus' Prophecy About Peter. Another objection to the doctrine of imminency stems from what Jesus told Peter, as recorded in John 21. He said, "When you were younger, you girded yourself and walked where you wished; but when you are old, you will stretch out your hands, and another will gird you and carry you where you do not wish" (v.18). This prophecy, which we know now indicated that Peter would be arrested and martyred, is used by some to refute the possibility of imminency. The return of Christ could not have been imminent because Jesus would have had to wait at least until Peter had passed from the scene at an old age.

Age is such a relative term. Does this mean Peter would have to be 75 before Jesus' words would be fulfilled? In the New Testament era, lifespans were much shorter than they are now. Paul, for example, called himself "aged" when he wrote to Philemon, and he was probably in his fifties. Taking into account that Peter was already in his mid-thirties when Jesus spoke those words, it would not be very many years until he too could consider himself old.

Granted, there would have been a few years in the first century during which anyone who knew of this prediction would have known that Jesus' coming was not imminent, but that time was brief. Besides, Peter was "old" by the time Paul wrote his epistles.

Now You See Them, Now You Don't

Several years ago, David Copperfield astounded a national television audience by making the Statue of Liberty "disappear." Those who watched the spectacle on TV confessed bewilderment and amazement at such a grand display of illusion. All the while, the audience knew, and Copperfield himself

agreed, it was all just a trick. The Lady never left her pedestal.

How that illusion by this master magician pales in comparison with what will occur when Jesus Christ appears to end this age and usher in the day of the

Lord! No mirrors, no stage hands, and no trickery will be needed when the Savior reaches out His arms and makes millions of people—both living and dead—disappear from earth.

Here's how Paul described the disappearance of millions into the heavens.

> *Behold, I tell you a mystery: We shall not all sleep, but we shall all be changed—in a moment, in the twinkling of an eye, at the last trumpet. For the trumpet will sound, and the dead will be raised incorruptible, and we shall be changed (1 Cor. 15:51-52).*

And in 1 Thessalonians 4:16-17 he said:

> *The Lord Himself will descend from heaven with a shout, with the voice of an archangel, and with the trumpet of God. And the dead in Christ will rise first. Then we who are alive and remain shall be caught up together with them in the clouds to meet the Lord in the air. And thus we shall always be with the Lord.*

From these two passages we can learn several things about the rapture.

Who Will Be Raptured? Imagine the thrill of hearing the shout of the Lord, the voice of the archangel, and the trumpet of God. Imagine looking up and seeing Jesus with His open arms, ready to hold you for an eternity. Imagine these things, though, only if you are a Christian. In both of these passages, Paul is addressing brethren, a term that denotes fellow believers in Jesus Christ. Also, in Paul's letter to the Thessalonians, he mentioned that the "dead in Christ" would rise first.

This indicates that all people who trusted in Jesus from the Day of Pentecost (the first time anyone was "in Christ") until the moment of rapture—both the living and the dead—would join Jesus. This is an event solely for Christians.

Will This Be A Secret Event? Some Bible students refer to this "catching up" of the church as a secret rapture. They claim that only Christians will hear the shouts and trumpet blasts. Whether or not this is true, this event will hardly be secret. When whole congregations of people disappear, when employees suddenly vanish, when vital public services are disrupted by mass absenteeism, people will notice. So no matter how blinded the unbelieving world may be to the events in the sky, they'll soon know that something extraordinary has occurred.

> The rapture will hardly be secret. When whole congregations of people disappear, when employees suddenly vanish, when vital public services are disrupted by mass absenteeism, people will notice.

What Happens To Believers? A quick trip to heaven is just the beginning of the marvelous things that will happen at the rapture. Apparently, the moment living believers are ushered into Christ's presence, they will receive their new bodies. Paul wrote, "We shall all be changed—in a moment, in the twinkling of an eye, at the last trumpet. . . . For this corruptible must put on incorruption, and this mortal must put on immortality" (1 Cor. 15:51-53).

Where Will Believers Go? Posttribulationists teach that when Jesus appears in the sky, Christians will rise to meet Him, make a U-turn, and descend to earth. Then Jesus will set up His earthly kingdom. Besides the obvious strangeness of this up-and-down scenario, this theory has another problem. It seems to contradict John 14. After Jesus had made the Upper Room announcement that He was departing, He reassured His disciples by telling them that His departure was related to what He was doing for believers—preparing an eternal dwelling place for them. Then He told them He would be coming back to take them to that place. If Jesus does not take us to be with Him at the rapture, then what happened to His promise of a place in His Father's house?

World Of Joy; World Of Terror

The rapture will change everything. In addition to calling out the world's population of Christians, it will create a new society of people with glorified bodies far removed from the limits of earth. No longer will this blue marble have a monopoly on the populace. And just as earth and heaven will be composed of  entirely opposite groups of people, so they will represent totally variant events. The two worlds will be as different as any two societies have ever been. Let's see what will be going on in these two divergent worlds in the years that separate the two stages of Jesus' return.

A Time Of Joy: An Awards Ceremony

Few scenes are as touching and heartwarming as the awards presentations at the Olympic games. We can all recall specific athletes and their reactions as they received their medal and then proudly turned to gaze upon their country's flag as the national anthem was played.

In a small measure, this can help us see what will transpire for the raptured believers at the event called the judgment seat of Christ (2 Cor. 5:10). Soon after Jesus has called His people together with a shout and a trumpet blast, this presentation of rewards will begin in heaven. Christians will stand before Christ the Judge, either to be rewarded with crowns (lit. a winner's wreath) for the good things they have done for God, or to "suffer loss" for their failure or neglect.

> Christians will stand before Christ the Judge and either be rewarded with crowns for the good things they have done for God or "suffer loss" for their failure or neglect.

To understand what it means to "suffer loss," think again of the Olympic athlete. The medalists earn the prize, while those who lose must step aside with the realization that they have not gained the reward. They are still members of their Olympic teams, of course, but they have suffered loss.

What, then, will be God's means of judging what was worthy of honor and what wasn't? First Corinthians 3:13-15 speaks of a trial by fire. Any works that were done with a selfish motivation will perish in the fire just as wood, hay, and stubble are consumed. But those things that were done on earth with God's glory in mind will live on. Like gold and silver, they cannot be burned. The key elements in testing these works will be their quality and the motivation behind them. What kind of rewards can the Christian work toward? At least five distinct crowns are mentioned in Scripture.

- An incorruptible crown for overcoming the old nature (1 Cor. 9:25-27).
- A crown of rejoicing for being a soulwinner (1 Th. 2:19-20).
- A crown of life for enduring persecution and trials (Jas. 1:12; Rev. 2:10).
- A crown of righteousness for eagerly looking forward to Christ's return (2 Tim. 4:8).
- A crown of glory for shepherding the flock of God (1 Pet. 5:4).

The glory of the event is only beginning when all the crowns are handed out, for these rewards are not earned for personal gain. When Christians receive their crowns at the judgment seat of Christ, they will give honor to Jesus by casting them at His feet (Rev. 4:10). Imagine the scene as millions of glorified believers offer their heavenly rewards to God for His glory!

A Time Of Terror: Antichrist And Judgment

What a contrast there will be between the best of times in heaven and the worst of times on earth! Although things may at first seem to be tolerable, after Jesus removes the Christians and the restraining power of the Holy Spirit, the situation will deteriorate quickly. Two events during this time will spell trouble, terror, and tragedy for those left behind. The first—the revealing of Antichrist—will precipitate the second—the tribulation.

Referred to as the "man of sin" in 2 Thessalonians 2:3, Antichrist will gain power as the final king of the restored Roman Empire. Of course, a man who achieves the measure of worldwide power that will go to Antichrist cannot do so without first conning his fellowman into following him. How he will do this is not exactly known, but he will probably show that he can create an orderly society out of one that has been reeling in chaos. In addition, he will work miraculous wonders by the power of Satan. Yet his benevolence will soon turn to malevolence. He will fiercely persecute and attempt to slaughter all who accept Christ and would dare refuse his demand that he be worshiped (Rev. 6:9-11).

Antichrist will not be the only source of suffering during this time of tribulation. In addition, these days will be marked by great calamity that will come as a result of God's judgment and wrath (Joel 1:15; Rev. 11:18; 16:9). Amid this devastation will be

> **Antichrist will not be the only source of suffering during this time of tribulation. These days will also be marked by great calamity—the result of God's judgment and wrath.**

the death of one quarter of the world's population (Rev. 6:8), massive earthquakes (Isa. 2:19), catastrophic fires (Isa. 24:1,3,6), and sudden destruction (1 Th. 5:3).

Near the last part of the great tribulation, Antichrist will unwittingly begin setting the stage for an event on God's prophetic calendar that will be the grandest event of all time—the revelation of Jesus Christ at His glorious return.

The King Is Back—To Stay!

The tensions that headline the nightly news from the Middle East in our day do not compare with the events that will mark the final months of action during the tribulation. As the clock winds down on the reign of Antichrist, more and more countries will align together against him and do battle with him in Palestine.

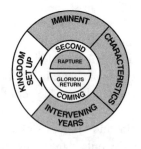

At the climax of those hostilities, armies of the "king of the north" and the "king of the south" will attempt to overrun Antichrist and his troops. Unfortunately for them and for the people of neighboring countries in the Middle East, Antichrist will lead his army to victory. As Daniel described it, "He shall enter the countries, overwhelm them, and pass through. He shall also enter the Glorious Land, and many countries shall be overthrown" (Dan. 11:40-41).

Yet all will not be calm in Antichrist's camp. Despite his victories, he will hear rumors that new armies from the Orient are ready to attack. Angrily, he will dispatch his troops to Jerusalem. Indeed, the Eastern armies will arrive, spelling trouble for the Jewish people. These new armies will stand against the Jews in Jerusalem—just as Antichrist's troops will. Here's how Zechariah described it:

> *I will gather all the nations to battle against Jerusalem; the city shall be taken, the houses rifled, and the women ravished. Half of the city shall go into captivity, but the remnant of the people shall not be cut off from the city (Zech. 14:2).*

The scene seems hopeless. The Jews have nowhere to turn as two opposing armies sweep over them. There appears to be no way out for this war-wracked people.

The Warrior-King Intervenes

Suddenly, the scene will change. The heavens will open and Jesus will return. He is portrayed as clothed in a robe dipped in blood and riding on a white horse as He appears in the air to send His white-clothed army against the armies of Antichrist (Rev. 19:11-21). Victory will be swift and complete as the beast is captured and banished to the lake of fire, and his army is soundly defeated.

> The King of the universe, who had appeared in the air just a few years before, will come back to end the tribulation and to establish His millennial kingdom on earth.

This, then, is the second coming of Jesus Christ. The King of the universe, who had appeared in the air just a few years before, will have come back to end the tribulation and to establish His millennial kingdom on earth.

The Judge-King Holds Court

Among Jesus' first duties as He prepares to set up His 1,000-year reign is to sit in judgment on several groups of people. Remember that He will have already judged many when He distributed rewards to the raptured saints after they were taken up to heaven. But now there are new people to examine. In the first days after our Lord's return to earth, He will judge three groups:

1. Resurrected believers from before Pentecost, along with martyred tribulation saints (Dan. 12:1-3).

2. Jews who had gone through the tribulation (Ezek. 20:33-44). Some will be allowed to become citizens of the kingdom and some will be cast into Hades. Their destination will depend on whether they chose to accept Christ or to follow Antichrist and his revolt.

3. Gentiles (Mt. 25). What Jesus will do with Gentiles who endured the tribulation will depend on how they treated Christ's "brethren" during those devastating years. Those who showed kindness to them showed their love for Jesus, so they will enter the kingdom. The rest will be "cast away" either because they worshiped Antichrist or because they mistreated Jews or both.

The Creator-King Re-creates

Shortly after Jesus' glorious return, He will transform this age-old earth, reversing some of the fallout from the curse in the Garden of Eden. These changes will allow the inhabitants of earth to enjoy a time of prosperity and happiness unparalleled in human history. His re-creation will be marked by:

Increased Productivity. Isaiah said that "the desert shall rejoice and blossom as the rose; it shall blossom abundantly" (Isa. 35:1-2). Evidently, new areas of land will be made fruitful, and this new source of usable land will lead to a time of great prosperity. Even the fishing will improve (Ezek. 47:9).

Better Weather. Notice again the words of Isaiah, who wrote, "Then He will give the rain for your seed with which you sow the ground, and bread of the increase of the earth; it will be fat and plentiful" (Isa. 30:23). Jesus' transforming work will include changes in the climate of earth. The sun will be more radiant, and even the moon will shine brighter (v.26).

Peaceful Coexistence Of Animals. "The wolf also shall dwell with the lamb, the leopard shall lie down with the young goat, the calf and the young lion and the fatling together" (Isa. 11:6-7). Although we don't know how this will affect such things as the food chain among animals, we can be assured that His plans for this time will surely cause our lives to be more enjoyable.

The Ruler-King Reigns

The millennial kingdom of our Lord Jesus Christ will not be a democracy. Rather it will be a benevolent dictatorship. Another way of describing it would be to call it a theocracy—a government led by God. As ruler of the earth during this time, Jesus will be a king who will "reign and prosper, and execute judgment and righteousness in the earth" (Jer. 23:5).

As King, Jesus will do what no other leader in history has been able to do. He will govern with absolute authority, righteousness, and justice. Finally, after so many failures on the part of mankind, a utopian world will have arrived. Jesus will rule as we have always desired leaders to rule.

Helping You Help Others

As you study the second coming with others, try using these questions as discussion starters. You'll find that digging into the Word will create a hunger for clear teaching and analysis of the topic.

Evidence For An Any-Moment Return

1. What biblical evidence suggests that Christ's return will be in two phases?
2. Why is the distinction between Israel and the church basic to understanding prophecy?
3. How can the following conflict be resolved? The Bible teaches that many dramatic events will precede the Lord's second coming, but it also predicts that Christ will come unexpectedly.
4. Why is it so important for us to live with the expectation that Christ could return at any moment? (2 Pet. 3:10-14; 1 Jn. 2:28–3:3).

Characteristics Of The Rapture

1. List as many characteristics as you can about the rapture of the church.
2. According to 1 Corinthians 15:51-53, what is in store for Christians who will be raptured?
3. How does Jesus' promise in John 14:1-3 that He would go to prepare a place for His followers fit into the rapture picture?

Christ's Return And You

Richard De Haan, former president and teacher of RBC Ministries, used to tell a story on himself that pictures the readiness Christians should have when they think of the rapture. When Richard and his brother Marvin were still living at home, their parents, Dr. and Mrs. M. R. De Haan would often have to go out of town for speaking engagements. The boys enjoyed the independence of being left alone—except for one thing. They detested doing the dishes.

On one such occasion, they put off sticking their hands in soapy dishwater as long as possible. They stacked the grimy plates, glasses, and silverware in the oven after each meal. Soon all the dishes were dirty and all the spare space was filled. Then, on the night before their parents were to return, Richard and Marvin rolled up their sleeves and had a marathon dishwashing session. Although the young De Haans never got caught with their dishes dirty, Richard commented, "How ashamed we would have been if our parents had come back earlier than we expected!"

The imminent return of our Lord Jesus should lead us to a similar sentiment. How ashamed we would be if He came back and we weren't expecting Him. Unlike our illustration, we do not know exactly when Jesus will return in the air to take His people to be with Him. As a result, we should live in a continual state of expectancy. We shouldn't be stacking our "dirty dishes"

> How ashamed we would be if Jesus came back and we weren't expecting Him.

all over; we should constantly keep our lives clean and in line with what God expects from us.

That's not the only part of our lives that should be affected by the hope of an any-moment return of our Lord. In addition, we should have a sense of urgency toward those who don't know Jesus. All too often we live as if we have all the time in the world to convey the message of salvation, when in reality we don't even know if we will have the rest of the day to do so. The prospect of lost opportunities to share the gospel should propel us into a deeper concern for the lost.

> The prospect of lost opportunities to share the gospel should propel us into a deeper concern for the lost.

Let's look at it another way. Suppose you knew exactly when Jesus would come back. You would probably have a "To Do" list that would fill pages:

- Write letters.
- Make phone calls.
- Pay back money owed.
- Apologize for wrongs done.
- Tell neighbors about Jesus.
- Pray for unsaved family members.
- Spend more time reaching out to the lost.

And on and on the list could go. More than anything else, we would want to get everything squared away before the big day that was coming closer every second. Although we would be secure in our salvation, we would want to do all we could to further the Lord's work in the time we had remaining.

The fact that we don't know the day and time of Jesus' return, though, shouldn't deter us from doing exactly that. We may not have the assurance that we can accomplish everything on that "To Do" list, but we should have those kinds of goals—perhaps with more urgency. Temporal goals lose some of their importance when we realize that we might not have as much time as we thought to accomplish things of eternal value.

There is another, even more important, consideration. Everyone who knows that Jesus Christ could come back at any moment must do some serious thinking. Beyond making lists of good things that need to be done, each person must make sure that he knows Jesus Christ as personal Savior. That is the single most important commitment any man, woman, or child could ever make.

> Temporal goals lose some of their importance when we realize that we might not have as much time as we thought to accomplish things of eternal value.

After Jesus returns for His own, those who have never accepted Him will be left behind to face a time of trouble and difficulty this world has never before seen. God's wrath will be poured out over the face of the earth. Death, destruction, deceit, and danger will reign. It's a prospect that should cause every thinking person to consider seriously the claims of Jesus Christ.

Yes, Jesus is coming back. Perhaps He will come today. Are you ready? If not, you can be. Without another second's delay, pray something like this: "Lord Jesus, I admit that I'm a sinner. I believe the Bible and what it says about You. Realizing that You gave Your life for me, that you died for my sins and arose from the dead, I am trusting You and You alone for my salvation."

That is the first and most important step in getting ready for His return, a return that may be today!

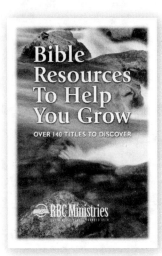